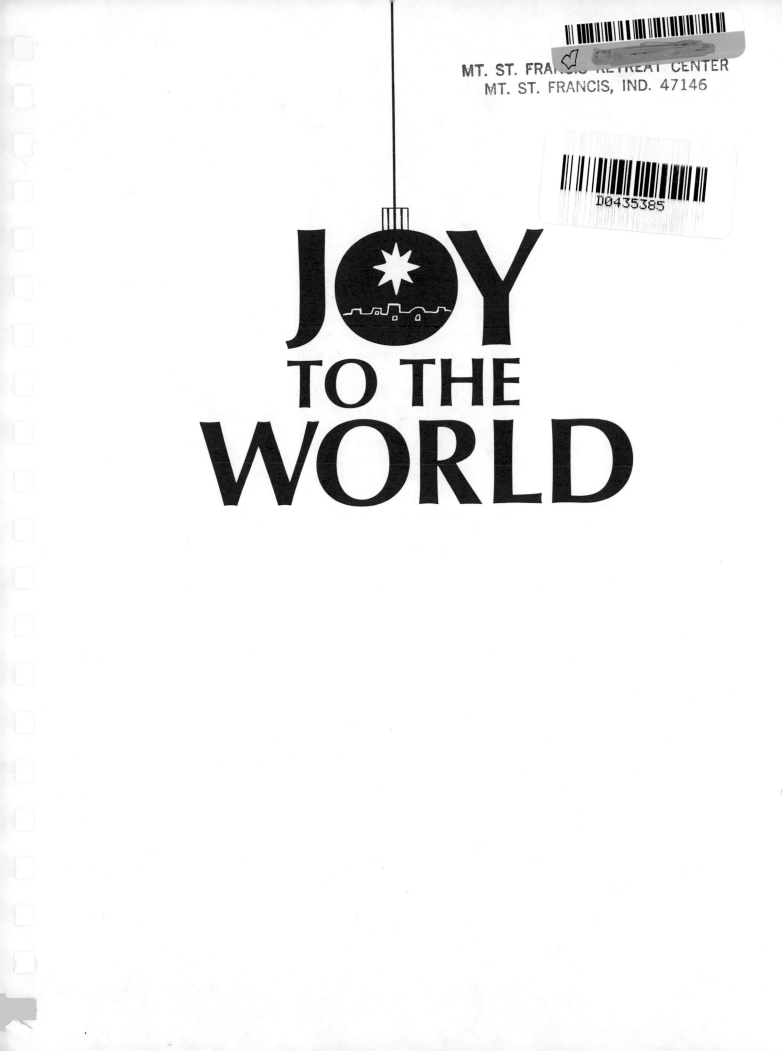

JOY
TO THE
WORLD

To Joyce and Ken Sherburn
. . . with gratitude to God for the gifts of
faith and friendship that we share. (PVW)

To my sisters and brothers
Carol Fournier Palmer
Dan Fournier
Don Fournier
Kay Fournier Reissig
Mary Fournier Toporski
Theresa Fournier
. . . your joys are a part of my life. (JDF)

Special thanks to
Ken, Stephanie, David, and Paul Wezeman

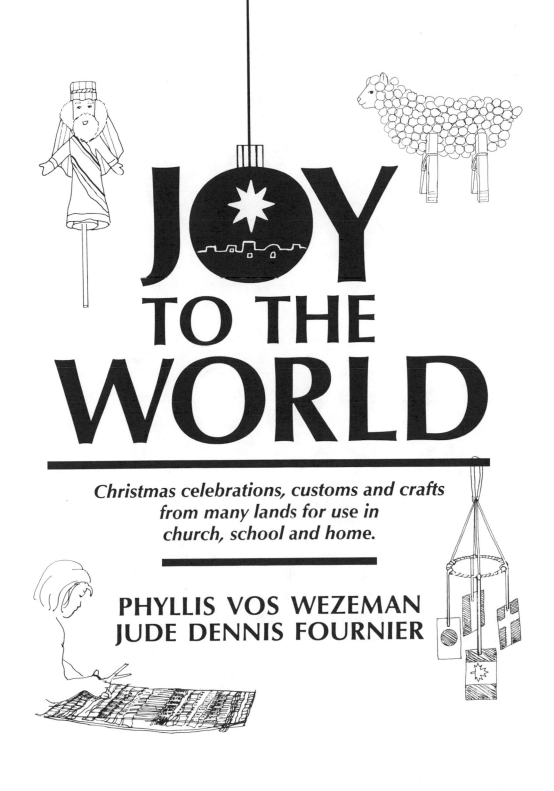

JOY TO THE WORLD

Christmas celebrations, customs and crafts from many lands for use in church, school and home.

PHYLLIS VOS WEZEMAN
JUDE DENNIS FOURNIER

AVE MARIA PRESS   Notre Dame, Indiana 46556

International Standard Book Number: 0-87793-489-4

Library of Congress Catalog Card Number: 92-71815

Cover, art, and text design by Katherine Robinson Coleman

Printed and bound in the United States of America.

▪CONTENTS▪

▪INTRODUCTION▪

Joy to the world!
The Lord is come:
Let earth receive her King.
Let every heart prepare him room,
And heaven and nature sing.

*T*he words of this familiar carol proclaim that Christmas is a worldwide celebration. Christians throughout the seven continents commemorate the birth of their Savior in countless ways: picnics on sunny beaches in Australia; Papai Noel delivering gifts to the children of Brazil; "Petit Jesu" sung in the French speaking sections of Canada; prayers offered during midnight masses in Ecuador; presents surrounding decorated trees in Germany; a profusion of poinsettia plants in India; printed postcards exchanged in Japan; posada processions moving through the villages of Mexico; clever verses that accompany gifts in the Netherlands; pageants that portray the nativity in Nigeria; puppet performances to delight children and adults alike in Poland; plates filled with delicacies from smorgasbord tables in Sweden.

Joy to the World is filled with activities designed to develop an awareness of and appreciation for the contributions that people of all lands and races make to the celebration of Christmas. The wealth of information about Christmas customs around the world offers readers a way to participate in a cross-cultural celebration of the feast. *Joy to the World* will help parents and children, teachers and students, pastors and parishioners recall that the Christ of Christmas came for all people of the world.

In the church year, the Christmas season is observed for twelve days — from December 25 to the feast of the Epiphany, January 6. Each of the twelve chapters in the book features a different country and contains twelve ways in which Christmas is celebrated there. Some countries have celebrated these Christmas customs for centuries, while in others the celebrations are as new as the Christian message itself. Through planning, preparing, and participating in the many projects suggested here, youth and adults can rediscover their own cultural heritage and grow to value the wealth of ideas and insights shared by others.

Each chapter contains several components. The following is an overview with suggestions for using each part.

Country Information

An overview of each country is provided at the beginning of the chapter. Share some of this information with participants as the events and experiences take place. Display a map of the world and of the nation being studied.

Refer to encyclopedias and other reference books for additional information on the countries. Some helpful resources include State Department Background Notes (Washington, DC: United States Department of State), and series such as *Enchantment of the World* (Chicago: Children's Books) and *Visual Geography* (Minneapolis: Lerner Publications). Contact embassies, consulates, travel agencies, and denominational mission boards for pamphlets, pictures, and posters.

If time and interest allow, you might want to review the information on the country by creating a collage or an ornament. Directions for both are suggested below.

Country Collage

Materials:

✦ Posterboard or construction paper   ✦ Scissors

✦ Pamphlets, magazines, newspapers   ✦ Glue

Method:

Create a collage for each nation, or one that includes all of the countries being celebrated. Find pictures that portray the people and places. Cut out the illustrations, arrange them as a group, and glue them to a piece of construction paper or posterboard. Cut out letters to spell the name of the nation and glue it on top of or over the pictures.

Map Ornaments

Materials:

✦ Map of country   ✦ Scissors

✦ Paper   ✦ Glue

✦ Pencil   ✦ Drapery ring

✦ Markers   ✦ String, yarn, or ribbon

Method:

Draw or reproduce a small map depicting the country being studied. Cut it to the size of a wooden or metal drapery ring. Glue the two pieces together. Loop a piece of string, ribbon, or yarn through the hook on the ring. Hang the ornament on a tree or wreath. Make one for each nation.

Flag

■

An illustration and description of each country's flag is given. Try to obtain an actual flag from a United Nations shop or other specialty store.

Make a flag for each country using a variety of materials such as construction paper, ribbon, paint, and trims. Attach the finished flags to string and make a garland or a mobile as suggested below.

Flag Garland

Materials:

- ✧ Construction paper
- ✧ Scissors
- ✧ Glue
- ✧ Pencil
- ✧ Ruler
- ✧ Markers
- ✧ Stapler and staples
- ✧ Paint
- ✧ Brushes
- ✧ String

Method:

For each flag, cut a paper rectangle in the background color. Cut the design from construction paper in the appropriate colors and glue it in place. You could also draw or paint the design on the background. Glue or staple the flags to a piece of string or ribbon. Use it as garland on a tree or as a room decoration.

Flag Mobile

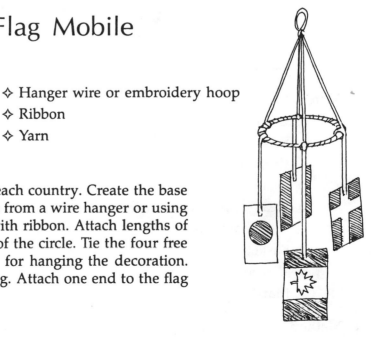

Materials:

- ✧ Construction paper
- ✧ Scissors
- ✧ Glue
- ✧ Hanger wire or embroidery hoop
- ✧ Ribbon
- ✧ Yarn

Method:

Construct a paper flag for each country. Create the base of the mobile by forming a circle from a wire hanger or using an embroidery hoop. Cover it with ribbon. Attach lengths of yarn to four equidistant points of the circle. Tie the four free ends together and make a loop for hanging the decoration. Cut a length of yarn for each flag. Attach one end to the flag and the other end to the hoop.

Greetings

The traditional greeting of the season is written in the official language of each country. Encourage the participants to learn to say and to write the phrases. Incorporate the greetings into a project such as a paper chain or a woven greeting.

Peace is also an important word for the Christmas celebration. The greeting of peace is given in the official language of each country. Use the ribbon banner or global greeting to help participants recall that the Prince of Peace was born at Christmas.

Directions for each of these project ideas are given below.

Paper Chains

Materials:

  ✧ Construction paper   ✧ Markers

  ✧ Scissors   ✧ Stapler

Method:

Cut the construction paper into strips of the desired length and width. Write the seasonal greeting for each country on a strip of paper. Make a loop of each strip and combine the pieces to form a paper chain. Add the completed chain to the Christmas tree as a way to recall that Jesus came for all people of the world.

Woven Greetings

Create a weaving to use as a picture or a wall hanging. Add pieces of material containing various greetings of the season to a frame after each country is celebrated.

Materials:

  ✧ Cardboard, 1 1/2' x 3', or large frame

  ✧ Scissors

  ✧ Cutting knife

  ✧ Heavy string

  ✧ Heavy yarns, cloth strips, wide ribbons, plastic bags, paper strips, or other such materials

  ✧ Basket or box

  ✧ 1" wooden slats. 1 1/2' or width of frame

  ✧ Marker

Method:

Prepare the cardboard by cutting one inch slits into the top and bottom of the piece. These should be placed approximately one inch apart. Warp the board by running a continuous piece of heavy string from one side to the other, through each slit.

Cut the materials into strips and place them in a basket or box. For each greeting, use a marker to write the words on a piece of material. Weave the strip into the warped cardboard. Periodically place a wooden slat into the weaving to make it more secure.

Display the finished product in a prominent place and continue to give thanks for the ways in which the customs of many cultures have combined to shape the season.

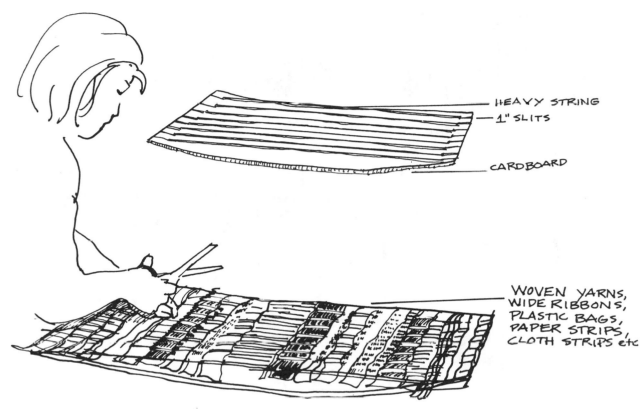

Ribbon Banner

Materials:

- ✧ Ribbon, 1" or wider
- ✧ Scissors
- ✧ Pole or rod
- ✧ Tacks or duct tape
- ✧ Permanent markers
- ✧ Basket or box

Method:

Choose ribbon to use for the activity. Cut it to the desired length and place it in a basket or box.

Write the greeting of peace for each country on a piece of ribbon. Tape or tack each ribbon to the pole or rod. Allow them to flow freely, or attach another pole across the bottom to make them more secure.

Display the banner. Remember the people in each country in prayer. Renew your commitment to working for justice and proclaiming the good news of the inner peace that Christ brings to the world.

Global Greeting

Materials:

- ✧ World map
- ✧ Index cards
- ✧ Markers
- ✧ String, yarn, or ribbon
- ✧ Scissors
- ✧ Push pins

Method:

Display the world map in a prominent place in the room. If possible, use a Peter's projection map, which illustrates the proportion of land area more accurately than the traditional Mercator projection map.

Write the peace greeting in the official language of each country on index cards. Prepare one card for each nation. Place the card on or around the map. Run a piece of string, yarn, or ribbon from the paper to the country location on the map. Use push pins to keep the pieces in place.

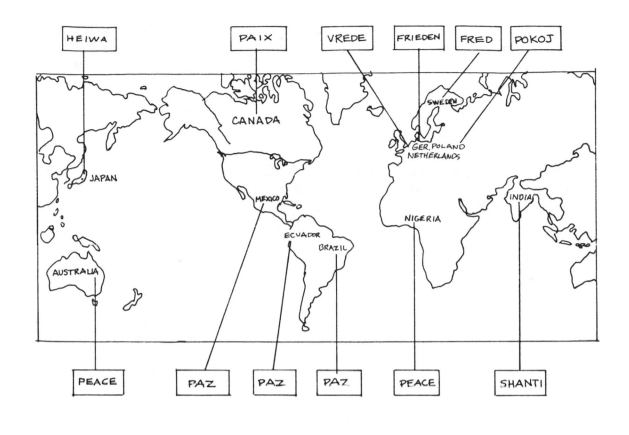

Customs

— ■ —

Many of the customs commonly associated with the celebration of the twelve days of Christmas are described in each chapter. Share some of them before the songs are sung, while crafts are constructed, or as treats are tasted. Try one of the following projects as a way of helping the participants discover more about the customs.

Video Box

Materials:

- Cardboard carton
- Knife
- Dowel rods
- Paper
- Markers
- Tape
- Cardboard or wood scraps

Method:

A video box combines a series of drawings that tell a story. The box may range in size from a tiny matchbox to a huge cardboard carton. The instructions below are for a large box that can display many drawings.

Begin by tucking in or cutting off the flaps of the carton. Use a mat knife to cut a large square out of the center of the bottom of the box. Leave a 2" to 3" border around the entire area. Turn the box on its side, so that the bottom now becomes the front, or viewing area.

Make a set of parallel holes in the top and bottom of the box on both sides of the window. Place a dowel rod through each set of holes. Secure them in place with tape or a cardboard or wooden stop.

Use markers to illustrate each custom on individual sheets of paper. When the drawings are completed, tape them together to form a long roll. Attach the beginning of the mural to one dowel rod and the end to the other. Wind the mural through the box to tell the story.

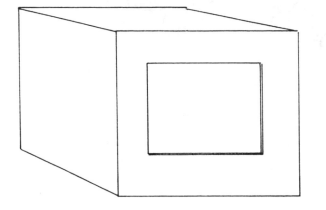
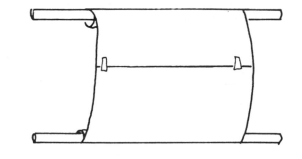
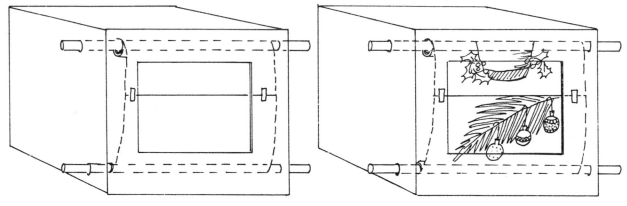

Slides

Make slides to illustrate the Christmas customs of various countries.

Materials:

✧ Acetate transparencies   ✧ Markers

✧ Slide mounts   ✧ Slide projector

✧ Scissors   ✧ Screen

Method:

Cut pieces of acetate transparency to fit the slide mounts. Draw a picture of a different tradition on each acetate. Put the slides in order. Use the projector to show the pictures on the screen.

Crèche

Information on the crèche, or nativity scene, traditionally found in each country is furnished. Instructions are provided for making a set of characters that reflect these traditions. Display the crèche in the classroom, home, or church.

Gift Giver

In every culture holiday gifts are presented by a special individual or group of people. Information on this is provided for each country. Help the participants remember the gift giver by making puppets or drawing overhead transparencies.

Tube Puppets

Materials:

✦ Paper towel tubes   ✦ Scissors

✦ Felt   ✦ Glue

✦ Yarn or fake fur   ✦ Craft sticks

✦ Fabric scraps

Method:

Turn paper towel tubes into puppets and use them to tell the story of the gift givers in various countries. Form the face by cutting a piece of felt and gluing it to the top one-third of the tube. Cut facial features, such as eyes, nose, and a mouth, from felt and glue into place. Use yarn or fake fur for hair. Attach it to the top of the tube.

Glue a piece of felt around the remainder of the tube to serve as an undergarment. Add layers of fabric in contrasting or complementary colors as overgarments. Cut an additional piece of material to make a head covering. Drape it over the hair and tie it into place with a piece of fabric or yarn. Make arms from strips of cloth or felt. Glue or sew them to the sides of the tube.

Apply a craft stick to the inside back of the tube to serve as the rod by which the puppet is operated.

Overhead Projector Pictures

Materials:

- ✧ Overhead projector
- ✧ Screen
- ✧ Acetate transparencies
- ✧ Permanent markers

Method:

Choose a gift giver and draw an illustration on an overhead transparency. Show the picture on the overhead projector and tell the story of the person. Make one for each country featured.

Card

Holiday greetings are exchanged throughout the world. Directions for making a Christmas card are included in each chapter. The instructions incorporate a technique that is common to the country.

Crafts

Suggestions for two crafts traditional to each country are given. Detailed directions for constructing the items are provided. The materials used are common items that can be easily obtained. Many of the crafts are ornaments that can be used as tree decorations or given as gifts.

Carols

Carols that originated in the country or that embody the spirit of a country's Christmas celebration are listed in each chapter. Find books cited in the references or other collections of hymns and carols at your church, library, or resource center. In some cases, verses are given in their original language as well as in English. Sing the carols suggested and find other songs from that region of the world.

Story

A story that describes the customs and traditions of each country is suggested and summarized. Find the book at a library, store, or resource center. Read the story as part of the celebration. The two activities suggested below can help the participants remember the message.

Flannelgraph Figures

Materials:

✧ Interfacing	✧ Glue
✧ Scissors	✧ Cardboard or thin plywood
✧ Markers	✧ Background material such as felt, flannel, or
✧ Patterns	indoor/outdoor carpeting
✧ Felt or sandpaper	✧ Stapler

Method:

Construct the background by covering the cardboard or plywood with felt, flannel, or indoor/outdoor carpeting. Staple the material in place.

Prepare patterns for the main characters of the book by cutting pictures from magazines or coloring books. Trace the figures onto the interfacing material. Color and highlight the pieces and cut them out. Back them with sandpaper or felt so they will adhere to the background material. Use the figures to illustrate the story.

Videos

Materials:

♦ Video equipment
♦ Costumes

Method:

Act out the message of the book. Dress in costumes, portray the characters, and video tape the story. Share it with a group.

Culinary

Two recipes for foods from the featured region offer a way to get a flavor of Christmas celebrations around the world. Celebrate the twelve days of Christmas by using the recipes to prepare a meal or a snack.

Game

Each chapter features a game related to the country. It may be one that is traditionally played by the people in that country, or it may be a game such as a word search or concentration, which can be used to review the country's Christmas customs.

Joy to the World can be used in a variety of ways in the church, school, home, and community. Pastors, teachers, parents, and children will find it a valuable resource for rediscovering the message and meaning of Christmas.

Congregations can use the material in worship, education, community life, and outreach. Some examples are: CCD or church school classes, supplemental or alternative curricula, youth groups, retreats, children's sermons, intergenerational events, weeknight education, holiday banquets, outdoor festivals, church school programs, after school care programs, children's church, sermon illustrations, family nights, women's or men's breakfasts, teacher training, vacation church school, summer programs, ecumenical events, and community festivities.

For an exciting educational program during Christmas break, invite the children to a "Christmas Around the World" event. Set up activity centers, sing Christmas songs, share holiday treats, and close with a worship service. You might also want to host a family night for the community.

Schools will benefit from using the material in the classroom as curriculum or for special projects. It is also appropriate for assemblies, worship services, days of reflection, pageants, and open houses.

Families can use this material for devotions or special commemorations. Highlight a different country during each of the twelve days of Christmas, or focus on one of the twelve parts of the chapter during each day of the season. A group of families might celebrate in homes with a round robin of Christmas activities. One family could prepare an array of Christmas songs and dances, another group might make the refreshments, the third household would share stories, the fourth stop might include time for crafts, and the evening could conclude with a prayer service at the last home.

Let the creative and challenging activities in *Joy to the World* help you explore, experience, and appreciate the contributions that all cultures make to the celebration of the birth of the Savior.

▪AUSTRALIA▪

Country Information

▬▬▬▬▬▬ ▪ ▬▬▬▬▬▬

*A*ustralia, a country about the size of the continental United States, is the world's smallest continent but one of its largest nations. The Commonwealth of Australia is located below southeast Asia and is bounded on the east by the Pacific Ocean and on the west by the Indian Ocean. Although the terrain is varied, most of the continent is low, irregular plateau. Since the country lies south of the equator, the seasons are opposite those of the northern hemisphere.

Almost seventeen million people live in Australia. Most are European of British background. A small percentage are Asians, and the remainder of the population consists of the original inhabitants, the Aborigines. The dominant religions are Anglican and Roman Catholic.

Australia has immense mineral and energy resources. It is one of the world's leading producers and exporters of aluminum, alumina, bauxite, cobalt, copper, industrial diamonds, gold, iron ore, lead, nickel, silver, and uranium. In addition, abundant supplies of coal, natural gas, liquid petroleum gas, and uranium make Australia a net exporter of energy products. Agricultural products include livestock, wheat, wool, and sugar.*

---

* Lorfano, Paula M., Editor. *Background Notes: Australia*. Washington, DC: United States Department of State, 1989.

Flag

The flag of Australia contains a blue field, and has the Union Jack of the United Kingdom in the top left corner. A large white star directly beneath the red Union Jack symbolizes federation, and five smaller white stars on the right half represent the Southern Cross constellation.

Greetings

The official language of Australia is English. The Aborigines also have their own native language. The Christmas greeting is the familiar *Merry Christmas*. The greeting of peace is simply *Peace*.

Customs

In spite of the vast difference in climate between cool Britain and hot Australia, Christmas celebrations in these geographically distant lands are remarkably similar. Although several of the Christmas customs observed in Australia were brought to the continent by early English explorers and settlers, throughout the years traditions unique to the "land down under" have emerged.

Since Australia is located in the southern hemisphere, Christmas occurs in the middle of summer. Scorching hot days and warm nights enable many holiday celebrations to take place outdoors. Children are on summer holiday from school and families travel to visit friends and relatives throughout the small continent.

Decorating the home begins several days before the holiday. People purchase plants and flowers, especially a Christmas bush and Christmas bell plants. Huge ferns and palm leaves are trimmed with ornaments. Green foliage is hung over the front door.

Caroling by candlelight is a distinctly Australian custom started by groups of mine workers. On Christmas Eve thousands of people gather in city parks to sing Christmas songs by the light of candles and torch flares.

On December 25, families gather around the breakfast table to exchange gifts. Following the fun and festivities they attend church. Christmas dinner is a meal of roast beef or fowl. The rest of the day might be spent at the beach, concluding with a picnic supper.

December 26, the second day of Christmas, is spent visiting family and friends and participating in sporting events.

Crèche

—■—

Shepherds and sheep are a significant part of the Christmas story. This must be especially meaningful to the people of Australia, one of the world's largest producers and exporters of wool.

Read Luke 2:8–20. Reflect on the fact that the shepherds were the first people to hear the good news that the Savior had been born. Create a crèche to use throughout the Christmas season by making simple sheep and figures from wooden clothespins. Easy directions are provided below.

Sheep

Materials:

- ✧ Posterboard
- ✧ Scissors
- ✧ Cotton balls
- ✧ Glue
- ✧ Clip clothespins, wooden
- ✧ Permanent marker, black
- ✧ Tempera or spray paint, black
- ✧ Bible

Method:

Cut the body of the sheep from posterboard. A pattern is provided on page 24. Use a black marker and draw a face on both sides of the posterboard form. Glue cotton balls to the remainder of the shape. Paint the clip clothespins black. When they are dry attach them to the bottom of the sheep to serve as legs. Construct several sheep and set them in and around the crèche.

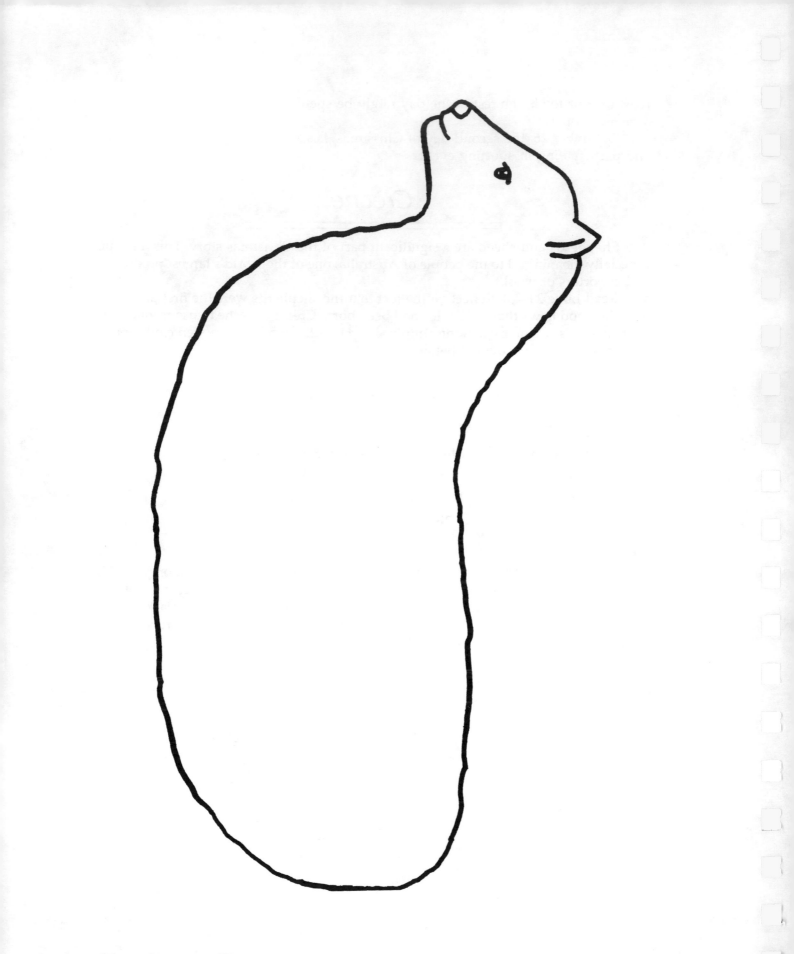

People

Materials:

- ✧ Wooden clothespins with rounded tops
- ✧ Pipe cleaners
- ✧ Fabric scraps
- ✧ Yarn
- ✧ Scissors
- ✧ Markers
- ✧ Shoe box
- ✧ Construction paper
- ✧ Straw or sand

Method:

For each figure, draw a face on the rounded top of the clothespin. Twist a pipe cleaner around the neck to form arms. Cut a 2" x 6" rectangle of fabric. Fold it in half and cut a small slit in the center. Slide the head through the opening. Arrange the material over the arms. Secure it in place by tying a piece of yarn around the middle. Use yarn glued to the top of the clothespin for hair. A small piece of cloth may be draped over the top of the head and tied in place with yarn.

Construct a variety of characters including Mary, Joseph, Jesus, shepherds, and angels.

Form the stable by covering a shoe box with construction paper. Set it on its side and sprinkle the bottom with straw or sand. Place the characters in and around it.

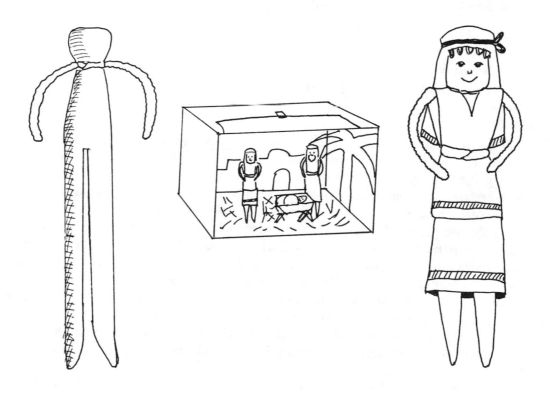

Gift Giver

—■—

Gifts in most areas of Australia are delivered by Father Christmas, the traditional British gift giver. The kindly old gentleman may arrive on water skis, in a rowboat, or riding an airplane rather than driving a sleigh.

In the Outback, Santa of the Spinifex, named for the scrubby brush that grows along his route, rides the Australian Commonwealth Railway system to bring gifts to the children.

Card

—■—

A hand-colored, printed greeting was designed by John Calcott Horsley in 1843 in England. This was the first Christmas card. Before this time, children in British schools made Christmas pieces to give to parents as a way to display improved penmanship. The practice of sending and receiving Christmas cards has now spread throughout the world. In Australia it is especially appropriate to send a greeting to a child or to an adult who has moved away.

Make a unique Christmas card by using the technique of sand painting (directions below) to illustrate an Australian holiday theme. Refer to the above customs for ideas.

Materials:

- ✧ Sand
- ✧ Tempera paint
- ✧ Newspaper
- ✧ Small bags
- ✧ Cardboard
- ✧ Posterboard or heavy paper
- ✧ Glue
- ✧ Scissors
- ✧ Paper
- ✧ Pencil

Method:

Begin by gathering sand from a beach, sandpit, or a building materials store. The sand can be colored by mixing a small amount of tempera paint into it and kneading it thoroughly. Spread the sand on newspaper to dry. Stir it from time to time to separate the particles. Pre-colored sand may also be purchased from a craft store. Place each color into its own small paper or plastic bag.

Sketch the picture for the card on a piece of paper. Try making a simple scene of a Christmas picnic on the beach, a Christmas bell plant, caroling by candlelight, or an Australian marsupial such as a kangaroo or a koala. Plan the colors of the project according to the materials that have been gathered.

Fold a piece of posterboard in half to serve as the card. Cut a piece of cardboard to fit the front of this card. Transfer the sketch to the cardboard.

Choose an area to be covered with a single color of sand. Spread white glue over the section. Sprinkle the desired color of sand over the glue. Allow the glue to dry.

Hold the cardboard over the bag or container from which the sand was taken. Tap the picture lightly so the loose sand falls into the bag.

Glue another small area and follow the same procedure. Continue until the painting is completed.

Glue or tape the sand painting to the front of the card. Write a Christmas verse inside. Follow an Australian custom by sending the greeting to a family member or friend who has moved out of the immediate area.

Crafts

The ideas below draw on the British heritage of many Australians. Crackers, English ornaments that are popular in Australia as well, are similar to favors used at birthday parties. The Christmas ones are often more ornate and may be filled with small candies, little toys, and papers with funny riddles written on them. Make several in different colors and sizes and use them to decorate a holiday tree. Share the contents with family and friends.

Pin prick pictures, a popular nineteenth-century English craft, combined with Australian holiday themes, can be made into Christmas ornaments. The background is painted with watercolors. Then the design is made by poking a pin, needle, or nail in and out of a piece of paper to create a pattern.

Crackers

Materials:

- ✧ Posterboard
- ✧ Scissors
- ✧ Glue
- ✧ Tape
- ✧ Tissue paper
- ✧ Christmas stickers or wrapping paper
- ✧ String or ribbon
- ✧ Candies
- ✧ Toys

Method:

For each "cracker," cut a 4" x 7" piece of posterboard. Roll it into a tube, overlapping the edges about one-half inch. Tape or glue the seam securely. Fill the tube with candies and toys. Seal each end with tape.

Make fringe for the ends from tissue paper. Cut two 4" x 8" pieces from two different colors of tissue paper. Fold each piece in half lengthwise. Starting from the folded edge, cut slashes approximately one-fourth inch apart, to within one-half inch of the unfolded edge. Open the tissue paper and turn it inside out. Wind one piece of each color of fringe around each end of the tube. Glue or tape them in place.

Decorate the tube with Christmas wrapping paper or stickers. Attach a piece of string or ribbon to each end of the tube and use this loop to hang the ornament on the tree.

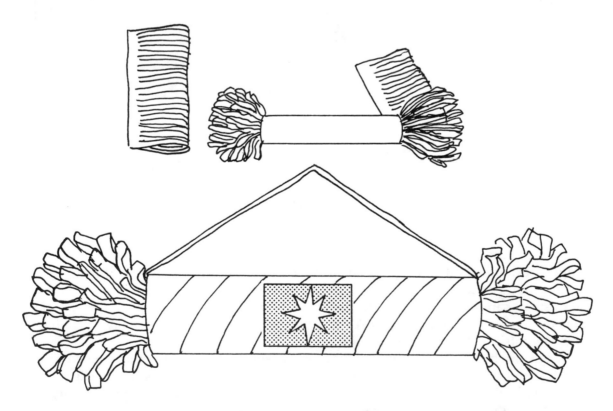

Pin Prick Pictures

Materials:

- Posterboard or heavy paper
- Scissors
- Pins, needles, nails
- Pencil
- Watercolor paints
- Brushes
- Water
- Canning jar ring, or metal or wooden curtain ring
- Glue
- Foam rubber
- Thread, string, ribbon, or yarn

Method:

Choose a subject for the scene, such as a person at the beach, a miner caroling by candlelight, a kangaroo, koala, sheep, or kookaburra bird.

Choose the frame for the ornament. Suggested materials include a canning jar ring or a metal or wooden curtain ring. Cut a piece of heavy paper or cardboard to fit inside of the frame.

If the background is to be colored, paint it with watercolor paints and allow the paper to dry thoroughly. Place the paper on a sheet of foam rubber and use pin pricks to design the picture. Various textures can be achieved by using different sized pins, needles, and nails. Vary the size of the holes by poking the implement part way or all the way through the paper.

When the picture is completed, glue it to the inside of the frame. Loop a piece of thread, string, yarn, or ribbon through the top of the picture to serve as a hanger for the ornament.Hang the pin prick picture on a traditional Christmas tree or place it on a potted palm or fern as the Australians might do.

Carols

Christmas caroling started in England in the Middle Ages when beggars wandered the streets during the holiday season singing for money, food, or drink.

"Carols by Candlelight" originated in Australia in the nineteenth century when Cornish miners left the copper mines on Christmas Eve and gathered by the light of their tallow candles to sing the seasonal songs of their homeland.

This event is celebrated on Christmas Eve or on one of the evenings in the week preceding Christmas. Thousands of people, each carrying a candle, gather outdoors to sing carols.

Carols such as "The First Noel" and "While Shepherds Watched Their Flocks" speak of sheep and shepherds, which is especially appropriate when learning about Australian Christmas customs.

Story

Australian illustrator Julie Vivas captures the spirit of the nativity story in a lovely picture book. The text uses excerpts from the King James Bible and the pictures illustrate the events that took place when the Savior was born.

Check in your library or a local bookstore for: *The Nativity*, Julie Vivas, illustrator (San Diego: Harcourt Brace Jovanovich, 1986).

Culinary

Since Christmas in Australia is celebrated in the summer, families and friends often spend the day at the beach. Barbecues, called barbies, are very popular for these picnics. People barbecue all kinds of meat, including lamb and fish. Hamburgers, called rissoles, and sausages or hot dogs, known as snags, would be served on damper (bread), with lots of tom sauce (catsup).

Try some foods with an Australian flavor during the twelve days of Christmas. One, the Wassail Bowl, is steeped in English tradition, while the other, Anzac, is a cookie from down under.

Wassail Bowl

A Wassail Bowl is served at buffets and festive gatherings throughout Great Britain and Australia. The name means "Be Thou Well" or "Be in Good Health."

Ingredients:

- ✧ 1 gallon apple cider
- ✧ 1/4 cup honey
- ✧ 1/2 to 2/3 cup lemon juice
- ✧ 1 six-ounce can frozen orange juice concentrate

- ✧ 4 cinnamon sticks
- ✧ 1 tablespoon whole cloves
- ✧ 1 tablespoon whole allspice
- ✧ 2 teaspoons nutmeg
- ✧ Cinnamon sticks for each cup (optional)

Method:

In a large pot, combine the cider, honey, lemon juice, orange juice concentrate, and four cinnamon sticks. Tie the cloves and allspice in a cheesecloth bag. Add this and the nutmeg to the cider. Cover and simmer for twenty minutes. Discard the cheesecloth bag and cinnamon sticks. Serve hot in mugs. Place a cinnamon stick in each mug.

Makes twenty-four servings.

Anzac Biscuits

Cookies are called biscuits in Australia. Anzac biscuits are traditional favorites.

Ingredients:

- ✧ 1 cup rolled oats
- ✧ 1 cup white flour, sifted
- ✧ 1 cup sugar
- ✧ 3/4 cup shredded coconut

- ✧ 4 ounces butter or margarine
- ✧ 2 tablespoons light corn syrup or molasses
- ✧ 1/2 teaspoon baking soda
- ✧ 1 tablespoon boiling water

Method:

Combine oats, sifted flour, sugar, and coconut.
Blend the butter or margarine with the syrup in a sauce pan.
Stir the mixture over low heat until melted and thoroughly blended.
Mix baking soda with boiling water and add to butter and syrup mixture.
Stir liquid mixture into dry ingredients until batter is formed.
Place teaspoons of batter onto a greased cookie sheet about three inches apart to allow for spreading.
Bake in a 350 degree oven for twenty minutes. Place biscuits on a rack to cool.

Game

———————— ■ ————————

Use a word search game to locate twenty words that describe highlights of the Australian Christmas celebration.

Locate twenty words that describe highlights of the Australian Christmas celebration. The words are hidden horizontally, vertically, and diagonally. Circle them as you find them. Words:

Summer	Outback	Gifts
Fruits	Bush	Kangaroo
Family	Father Christmas	Barbeques
Koala	Sports	Church
Candlelight	Caroling	Sheep
British	Aussies	Plants
Picnics	Beaches	

```
Z D X N Y Q N V J I X Z S S M V S T D D
P V Y L I M A F T O A A V U X U Q S M N
M D P I C N I C S T K V S A V Y P H Y W
W C C G Y S M O U T B A C K H R S R O P
S K U Y I P N K P X G P U Z S N Q X Z Y
U G Z S A M T S I R H C R E H T A F S V
Y E K R A R Y R B J K S Q B S I A A E X
Y C A R O L I N G M U S A P Q K B L O S
S T X S D A T D M C R O M C K I T E H
Q A Y T J H A H M E B R M J O Z Z H I P
Z L H F V H E E H E T B P Q O U C U R D
V A S I I S R E Q S W X R Z C A Z G G Z
T O U G T J O U P F I O U I E H O J O B
C K B N C Z E Q O I D R T B T Q U L C Z
B O A T U S K A N G A R O O F I E R L Q
P L D I M P H F U D G J N T R R S O C K
P C A N D L E L I G H T C B U W B H V H
V V S E I S S U A M X C C D I O Z R N S
X O C F V M F E X S Q K W R T P M G W T
V Z W G Z W Q K G B U Z P G S K C F X C
```

Answer Key:

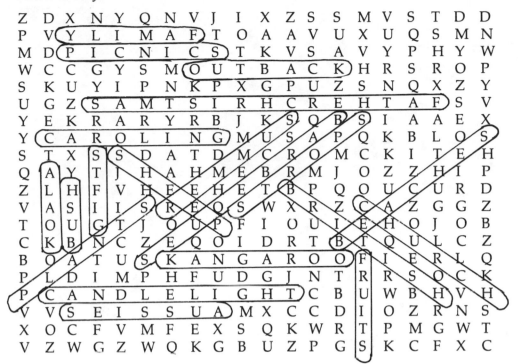

▪BRAZIL▪

Country Information

▬

*B*razil, the most populous country in Latin America and the sixth largest in the world, has a population of over 150 million people. Four major groups make up the Brazilian population: indigenous Tupi and Guarani Indians: the Portuguese, who began colonizing in the sixteenth century; Africans brought to Brazil as slaves; and various European and Asian immigrant groups including people from Italy, Germany, Spain, Japan, Poland, and the Middle East. Brazil is the only Portuguese-speaking nation in the Americas.

Ninety percent of the population belongs to the Roman Catholic church. The other ten percent are Protestants of various denominations and spiritualists.

Brazil's climate is tropical or semi-tropical. The terrain varies from dense forests in northern regions; semi-arid areas along the northeast coast; mountains, hills, and rolling plains in the southwest, and a coastal strip.

The Federative Republic of Brazil is rich in resources. About one-half of the land is covered by various types of forests. Natural resources include iron ore, bauxite, nickel, uranium, gemstones, and oil. Brazil is the world's leading exporter of coffee and orange juice concentrate, the second largest exporter of cocoa and soybeans, and a major exporter of sugar, meat, and cotton.*

---

* Adams, Juanita, Editor. *Background Notes: Brazil.* Washington, DC: United States Department of State, 1990.

Flag

Brazil's flag is a green field with a yellow diamond in the center. The green and yellow signify forest and mineral wealth. A blue globe in the center of the diamond shows twenty-three white stars and a band with "Ordem e Progresso" written on it. The globe represents the sky and the vastness of the states and capital.

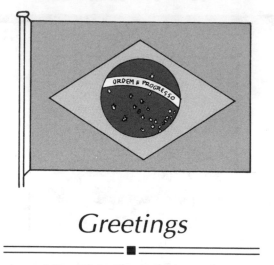

Greetings

The official language of Brazil is Portuguese. The Christmas greeting is *Boas Festas*. The greeting of peace is *Paz*.

Customs

Brazil is a melting pot of many races and ethnic heritages, resulting in a rich kaleidoscope of customs. Since the holiday occurs in the summer, many of the festivities take place outdoors. Christmas Day may be celebrated at the beach with picnics, swimming, boating, and fireworks. Open-air dancing and caroling take place before the midnight mass.

Misa de Gallo, the Mass of the Cock, is a time of worship at midnight on Christmas Eve. Since over ninety percent of the country is Catholic, the service is well attended. After church, families gather for a festive meal that often includes roast pig or fish pie.

Decorations feature bright flowers and ripe fruits. Sometimes a tree is covered with cotton to resemble snow. Crèches are often elaborate scenes that fill one or more rooms of a home. Besides depicting the holy family in Bethlehem, they may also have a train set running around it or a toy airplane flying overhead to suggest the modern world.

A common custom re-enacts Mary's ride through Bethlehem. A woman rides a donkey through the village as part of the Christmas celebration.

On January 6, Three Kings' Day, poetry contests are held in many areas and the verses are sung to guitar accompaniment.

Crèche

— ■ —

Brazilian crèches are generally composed of carved or clay figures. They often use brightly colored sawdust as the base material. The figure of the infant Jesus is placed in the manger on Christmas Eve, and the wise men are moved closer to the scene every day.

The prayer service below celebrates the Christmas crèche in the spirit of the Brazilian people.

Materials:

- ✧ Incense
- ✧ Incense container
- ✧ Recorded music
- ✧ Tape, record, or CD player

Method:

Opening Song: "Silent Night"

Gathering Prayer

Leader: God of birth and of new life, we come here today to celebrate Christmas, the feast of the incarnation. Help us to fully experience this holy night. May Jesus the Messiah be birthed in our hearts. Send us your Spirit that we might be still, that we might seek silence, that we might find peace among the stars. On this most blessed of nights, a Savior has been born; Emmanuel, God with us. We ask your blessing.

All: Amen.

Proclaiming the Word (a dramatic reading for three voices)

One: "Fear not," said Yahweh, the eternal one. "Be comforted my people and be filled with peace."

Two: "In a time long ago I molded and formed you, naked in your mother's womb. I have heard your cries. I am your God and I shall not leave you alone. You are my people!"

Three: Oh pilgrims of Yahweh your God,
sing your holy songs,
and be filled with peace.
For this most sacred night
has been made for you —
the awaited time,
the moment of Redemption's entry.
Seek stillness,
for peace is found in the midst of humanity.

One: Yahweh, the eternal one, looked with favor upon her, a child pure, untouched by life, holy, blessed among all people. And Yahweh cared for her with a loving hand. The eternal one protected her from harm's way, preparing her for a holy birth — Emmanuel, God with us.

Two: A human vessel held the living Word. Incarnation: God with us. Vulnerable, young, she said yes. She risked for her God and for the whole of creation. They traveled in darkness, trusting the mystery.

Three: Oh pilgrims of Yahweh your God,
sing your holy songs,
and be filled with peace.
For this most sacred night
has been made for you —
the awaited time,
the moment of Redemption's entry.
Seek stillness,
for peace is found in the midst of humanity.

One: Mary and Joseph, weary with travel came to a barnyard door. It was the only place. No room here, no room there. It was census time. Only a bed of straw was left. The sky filled with stars, the animals comforted, the doves sang, shepherds watched by night. All was calm.

Two: A young woman lays on the barnyard floor. The time of birthing is at hand. Tender eyes gaze toward the sky. Deep breaths of spirit life — in and out groans from the virgin one. Upon a hard floor of wood and nails the Messiah comes forth from the womb of the virgin.

Three: Oh pilgrims of Yahweh your God,
sing your holy songs,
and be filled with peace.
For this most sacred night
has been made for you —
the awaited time,
the moment of Redemption's entry.
Seek stillness,
for peace is found in the midst of humanity.

One: She wrapped him in swaddling clothes, and laid him in a manger. She had brought forth her firstborn son. And the shepherds came with great haste, and found the holy family, and were no longer afraid.

Two: Yes, a child is born unto us, and the world shall be upon his shoulders; and his name shall be called Wonderful, Counselor, Mighty God, Eternal One, Prince of Peace. All shall come and adore Emmanuel, the long awaited one. Women and men, children, people of all ages, look with open eyes. God made flesh. This coarse reality of incarnation. The promises of this holy night.

Three: Oh pilgrims of Yahweh your God,
sing your holy songs,
and be filled with peace.
For this most sacred night
has been made for you —
the awaited time,
the moment of Redemption's entry.

Seek stillness,
for peace is found in the midst of humanity.

Ritual Action

During a brief silent time, prepare a bowl with incense. Move through and around those gathered, carrying the bowl of incense as a sign of the Holy Spirit and as a means of purification. Play soft Christmas music during this time.

Blessing

Leader: As a sign of our belief in God and in the Word made flesh, let us ask for one another a blessing, "*Bencao*." Please extend your hands over each other and offer a prayer.

Closing Prayer

Leader: We give you thanks, Gentle One, for having touched our souls. You have loved us through all of time. You redeemed us through Jesus. We ask you now to bless us, to bless the people of Brazil, to bless all our world.

Closing Song: "Good Christian Friends, Rejoice"

Gift Giver

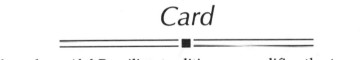

Since homes in Brazil seldom have chimneys, Papai Noel, the gift giver, is said to enter through the window. Even though Christmas is celebrated in the middle of summer, Papai Noel arrives in black boots and a red flannel suit. Children leave their shoes under the Christmas tree to be filled with toys and treats.

Card

White gifts, a beautiful Brazilian tradition, exemplifies the true spirit of Christmas: it is better to give than to receive. Introduced many years ago by missionaries, the custom involves giving white foods such as potatoes or rice, so that the poor may have Christmas dinner.

During the midnight mass, *Misa de Gallo*, people of all ages, races, and economic backgrounds, walk to the front of the church to place their gifts in a crude manger filled with straw. All of the packages are wrapped in white paper. A small light shines in the manger to symbolize the light of Christ.

The instructions below tell how to make a card that depicts this Brazilian custom.

Materials:

- ❖ Paper, white
- ❖ Glue
- ❖ Ribbon, white
- ❖ Marker
- ❖ Magazines
- ❖ White foods
- ❖ Scissors

Method:

Fold a piece of white paper in half to form a card. Design the cover of the card in one of the following ways.

1. Cut pieces of white ribbon the length and the width of the front of the card. Glue them in place to resemble a wrapped package. Place a small white bow in the center.

2. Cut or tear paper to represent the manger that is placed in front of the church on Christmas Eve to receive the presents. Fill it with white gifts that are cut or torn from paper of another texture.

3. Make a collage of white foods such as potatoes, rice, cheese, milk, eggs, fish and turkey and glue pictures that have been cut from magazines to the front of the card.

On the inside of the card, write a paragraph about the tradition of white gifts. Give the card, along with a gift of white food, to a family in need or to an agency that distributes food baskets to people during the Christmas season.

Crafts

—■—

Crafts from Brazil reflect the influence of the country's native, European, and African inhabitants. Bold sculpture, beautiful carvings, and brilliant paintings are found both indoors and outside.

Directions are provided for two craft projects, tissue paper flowers and painted rocks, that will serve as reminders of the culture and customs of Brazil. The flowers suggest the bright blossoms that bloom during the holiday season. The rock activity suggests the beach festivities of many Brazilians.

Tissue Paper Flowers

Make several of these flowers in different colors and sizes, and use them as table or tree decorations.

Materials:

◇ Tissue paper, various colors   ◇ Florist wire

◇ Scissors   ◇ Floral tape, green

Method:

Trace the patterns on page 42 and enlarge or reduce to the desired size. Cut the petals from various colors of tissue paper. For a fuller flower, cut two or three of each petal. Put the decorations together in order, with number one as the base of the flower.

Cut a piece of florist's wire 12" long. Beginning underneath the base of the flower, run the wire up through the center of all the petals, then back down in the center to form a small loop. Twist the two pieces of wire together and cover the stem with green floral tape.

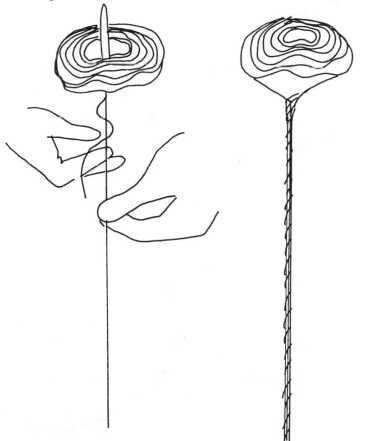

Painted Rocks

Materials:

- ◇ Rocks
- ◇ Acrylic paints
- ◇ Brushes
- ◇ Paper
- ◇ Pencil

Method:

Choose smooth, flat rocks to use for this activity. They may be any size and are available from beaches, gardening centers, landscape architects, and construction suppliers.

Sketch a picture associated with one of the Christmas customs of Brazil. It could be a white gift, a colorful flower or a native food. Paint the design on one or both sides of the rock and use it as a paperweight or table decoration. Make several and give them as gifts.

Carols

In many homes families gather during the holiday season to sing Christmas songs and hymns. The beloved Bavarian carol "Silent Night" is a favorite among Brazilians of German heritage. Another favorite carol is "Good Christian Friends, Rejoice."

Story

As the tree is trimmed in Brazilian homes on Christmas Eve, the parents tell the Christmas story in words simple enough for even the youngest child to understand.

Read the scripture passage (Lk 2:1–20) from different versions of the Bible and from a variety of Bible story books.

Culinary

On Christmas Eve in Brazilian homes, the dinner table is prepared before the family attends midnight mass. This tradition is kept so that the holy family can eat if they visit while the service is taking place. A holiday meal might consist of roasted pig served with a steamed fish pie made of corn meal, cassana flour, sardines, and shrimp.

Recipes for one traditional Brazilian dish, *feijoada*, and one festive dessert, anthill cake, are offered below.

Feijoada

Recipes containing beans are common in Brazil. Meat, such as ham or pork, may be added to this recipe. Ingredients:

- ◊ 1 large onion
- ◊ 1 clove garlic, minced
- ◊ 2 tablespoons salad oil
- ◊ 1 bay leaf
- ◊ 1 cup black beans or small red beans
- ◊ 3 1/2 cups water
- ◊ 1/2 teaspoon coriander seed
- ◊ 1/4 teaspoon pepper
- ◊ One half orange
- ◊ 2 stalks celery, chopped
- ◊ 3 tablespoons tomato paste, or one fresh tomato, chopped
- ◊ Rice
- ◊ 1/4 cup bread crumbs, toasted

Method:

In a large pot, cook the onion and garlic in the oil until tender. Add the water, beans, and bay leaf. Cover the pot and soak the beans overnight. After the beans have soaked, add the coriander, pepper, orange half, celery, and tomato. Cover and simmer for two to three hours, stirring occasionally. Add water if necessary. Remove bay leaf before serving.

Serve the bean mixture over cooked rice. Prepare one cup of raw rice for each recipe of beans. Top with toasted bread crumbs.

Makes six servings.

Anthill Cake

Pieces of chocolate and coconut form the "ants" in this rich, dense cake. Although the original recipe calls for coconut milk, regular milk may be used.

Ingredients:

- ◊ 2 cups sugar
- ◊ 2 cups flour
- ◊ 1 cup cornstarch
- ◊ 1/2 cup unsweetened grated coconut
- ◊ 1 tablespoon baking powder
- ◊ 4 egg yolks
- ◊ 1 cup milk or coconut milk
- ◊ 1 cup margarine, melted
- ◊ 4 egg whites
- ◊ 1/4 — 1/3 cup semi-sweet chocolate, grated
- ◊ Salt
- ◊ Powdered sugar

Method:

Mix together the sugar, flour, cornstarch, grated coconut, and baking powder. Combine the egg yolks, milk, and melted margarine. Mix the dry and liquid ingredients together. Beat the egg whites to stiff peaks and fold into the mixture. Add the chocolate pieces and a pinch of salt. Mix gently.

Preheat the oven to 350 degrees. Pour the batter into a greased and floured pan. A Bundt pan works the best, but an angel food pan or a standard 13" x 9" cake pan may also be used.

Bake 45–60 minutes. Top should be golden brown and toothpick inserted in the center should come out clean. When cool, sprinkle with powdered sugar.*

Game

Ferol Bola is a favorite game of Brazilian children. You can make the equipment from readily available materials. The game can be played in warm or cold weather.

Materials:

- ✧ Two wooden paddles,
  a bit larger than ping pong paddles
- ✧ Paint
- ✧ Brushes
- ✧ Large cork
- ✧ Feathers
- ✧ Rope or chalk

Method:

Paint bright, colorful pictures on each of the two wooden paddles. Scenes of holiday celebrations in Brazil would be appropriate. Decorate a large cork with feathers. Use a rope or chalk line to mark the center of the playing area on a lawn, sidewalk, or beach.

The object of the game, much like badminton, is to hit the cork back and forth over the center line without letting it fall to the ground. Keep score. The first person to reach ten points plays a new partner.

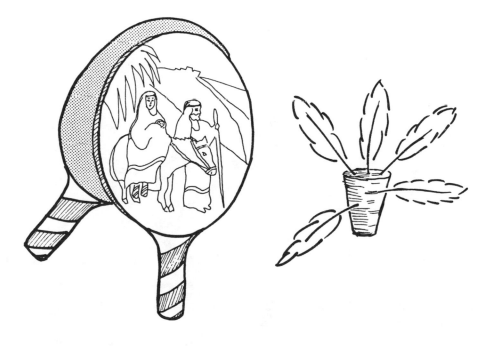

* Schlabach, Joetta Handrich. *Extending the Table. . . A World Community Cookbook*. Scottdale, PA: Herald Press, 1991, p. 306. Used by permission.

▪CANADA▪

Country Information

▪

Canada, located on the North American continent, is nearly four million square miles in area and is the second largest country in the world. It shares over five thousand miles of its southern border with the United States. Canada's ten provinces and two territories vary greatly in population, ethnic composition, industry, terrain, and climate.

The Atlantic provinces (Newfoundland, Prince Edward Island, Nova Scotia, and Ne Brunswick) consist of rounded hills and rolling prairies. Primary industries are fishing, agriculture, mining, and manufacturing.

Quebec, an area in which agriculture, mining, manufacturing, and hydroelectric power plants are found, has a terrain of fertile, low-lying plains. Quebec began as a French trading post, and most of the people who settled there came from France. Ontario, a highly populated region, is a manufacturing, agricultural, and mining tract.

The prairie provinces (Manitoba, Saskatchewan, and Alberta) are famous for their wheat fields and ranches. The area called the Canadian Shield is a vast wilderness with thick forests, wildlife, thousands of lakes, and natural resources including large deposits of oil, gas, and coal.

British Columbia, the Yukon Territory, and the Northwest Territory are a mountainous region known for forestry, manufacturing, fishing, mining, and agriculture.

One quarter of Canada's twenty-six and a half million people are British, another quarter are French, and the remaining inhabitants are generally of German,

Ukrainian, Scandinavian, Italian, Dutch, Polish, indigenous Indian, or Eskimo (Inuit) origin.

The official languages of the country are English and French.*

Flag

On Canada's flag a red maple leaf on a white background is flanked by red vertical bands.

Greetings

Since English and French are both official languages of Canada, the greetings of the season are *Merry Christmas* and *Joyeux Noel*. The greeting of peace is *peace* or *paix*.

Customs

Although Christmas is celebrated in a variety of ways throughout Canada, the information in this chapter pertains to the French influence found mainly in the province of Quebec. Signs that Christmas is approaching begin after the appearance of Saint Nicholas on December 6, and celebrations continue through Epiphany (January 6), which celebrates the visit of the wise men.

Specialty stores offer a wide variety of decorations. While cut trees can be found at outdoor markets, potted ones are often preferred since they last longer and can be planted out-of-doors after the holiday season concludes. Flower stands are filled with plain or flocked branches of fir, boughs of holly, and sprigs of mistletoe. The most important decoration is flowers. Favorites are fresh roses, gladioli, carnations, snapdragons, red and white poinsettias, hyacinths, azaleas, and begonias. The Christmas rose and dried flowers make lovely holiday centerpieces.

---

* Adams, Juanita, Editor. *Background Notes: Canada*. Washington, DC: United States Department of State, 1989.

A few days before Christmas the tree is put up, but it is not lighted until December 25. If candles are used, they are generally red.

Crèche scenes, filled with *santons* ("little saints"), are found in homes, churches, and public places. Besides the traditional nativity characters, people from all walks of life are depicted in the elaborate models.

Preparations for the Christmas Eve supper, called *reveillon*, begin several days in advance. Shopping for the meal takes place at the fruit stand, butcher shop, open air fowl market, pastry shop, fish house, cheese and pâté shop, bakery and candy shop.

Before *reveillon* begins, the family attends the midnight mass. In most churches the beautiful carol "O Holy Night" is sung at the stroke of midnight. At home, the figure of the infant Jesus is placed in the manger.

On this night, children leave their shoes for Pere Noel to fill with treats. In the morning, or after *reveillon*, the young people open their gifts of toys, games, and candy.

New Year's Day is an occasion for visiting family and friends. Another *reveillon* is held. This one is given by the oldest member of the family and all relatives are invited. Adults receive gifts of flowers, perfume, jewelry, or books and children are given money on this holiday.

January 6, Epiphany, concludes the season of Christmas and includes the tradition of the cake of the kings (*galette des rois*). A bean or a small porcelain figure of the baby Jesus is baked inside and the person who finds it becomes ruler for the day.

Crèche

In 1223 Saint Francis re-created the events of Christ's birth with a live nativity scene in the hills near Assisi, Italy. After he filled a manger with hay, surrounded it with real animals and placed a wax image of the baby Jesus into the crib, he told the Christmas story to the villagers and shepherds. The custom of the crèche spread to other countries and appeared in France between 1316–1334.

In the early 1800s, Italian peddlers traveling through southern France sold small clay figures to the villagers. The French people were so delighted with the statues that they began to make their own. At Christmas time terra-cotta figures, called *santons*, were made for the crèche scenes.

These colorful characters now come in two varieties, clay figures that are hand painted and clay figures that are clothed. Many sizes are available.

In homes, churches, and public buildings throughout the French-speaking areas of Canada ornate crèches are constructed. Figures representing people from everyday life — the mayor, priest, policeman, butcher, baker, even thieves and convicts — are depicted, in addition to the traditional figures from the nativity story. Each of them has a special gift to offer to the Christ child. It may be fruit, flowers, chicken, or cake. The manger remains empty until Christmas Eve, at which time the figure of "Little Jesus" is lovingly placed into the crib.

Construct and display items representing the Christmas story and present them in a table top model in the home or church.

Materials:

- Bible
- Construction paper scraps
- Fabric scraps
- Pipe cleaners or chenille wires
- Cardboard pieces
- Crayons, markers, or paints
- Brushes
- Scissors
- Glue
- Tape

Method:

Read the Christmas story found in the Bible (Lk 2:1–20). Make a list of the traditional characters to include in the model. Instead of using clay, form the figures of people and animals by bending and shaping pipe cleaners. Add fabric and construction paper scraps to make faces and clothing.

In keeping with the French Canadian tradition of including people from all walks of life in the crèche, brainstorm a list of historical or modern day persons to place in the scene. Remember that the Christ child welcomes all people and be sure to include rich and poor, old and young, sick and well. Depict people from different countries in the crèche too. Make these characters from pipe cleaners and decorate them with a variety of materials.

Place the figures on the top of a table. Decide on the type of scene that will surround the "santons" and create it from materials with interesting textures and shapes. Add trees, hills, water, buildings, and anything else that would enhance the model. Enjoy the scene during the twelve days of Christmas.

Gift Giver

At one time French Canadian children believed that Petit Jesu, or Little Jesus, personally visited homes and delivered gifts and treats on Christmas Eve. Later the gift giver was called Petit Noel, or Little Christmas. Today most children believe that Jesus sends Pere Noel in his place.

Pere Noel, or Father Christmas, is a tall, slender old man with a white beard who wears a long red robe that is edged with white fur. As he travels from place to place he cries "Tralala, tralala, bouli, bouli, boulah." Pere Noel carries a sack of toys and is often accompanied by a donkey.

If there is a fireplace in the home, children place their shoes, slippers, or boots near it on Christmas Eve. Shoes may also be set near the Christmas tree or the crèche if there is no fireplace. Children often leave a snack for Pere Noel and food for his donkey as well.

On Christmas morning the shoes are hidden in a pile of brightly wrapped gifts. Adults exchange presents on New Year's Day.

Card

Stained glass is an artform in which pieces of tinted glass are assembled in a lead frame to form a picture or design. Daylight or artificial light that passes through the glass is transformed into an array of colored light.

Stained glass windows, found in the great cathedrals of the world, often depict scenes from Bible stories. Topics related to the Christmas story include the madonna and child, the holy family, the adoration of the shepherds, and the visit of the magi.

The directions below will tell you how to make a Christmas card that resembles a stained glass window.

Materials:

- ✧ Construction paper, black and white
- ✧ Tissue paper, various colors
- ✧ Scissors
- ✧ Glue
- ✧ Tape, masking or transparent
- ✧ Paper punch
- ✧ String

Method:

To make the stained glass design, begin with a square of black construction paper. Fold the square corner to corner to form a triangle. Cut a circle out of the paper. With the black paper still folded into the triangle shape, or smaller, cut a design such as a star or a snowflake. Remember to cut on the folds as well as on the edge of the black. Glue or tape colored tissue paper behind each opening of the design.

Fold a piece of white construction paper in half and glue the stained glass piece to the front. Write a message on the inside of the card before it is delivered or mailed.

Crafts

—■—

Christmas markets throughout Canada feature special stalls displaying countless varieties of holiday decorations. Department stores are filled with treasures and trinkets as well. Families add new ornaments to their trees every year. Below are directions for two handmade ornaments.

Pine Cone Ornaments

Materials:

- ⬦ Pine cones   ⬦ Paint
- ⬦ Scissors   ⬦ Paint brushes
- ⬦ Glue   ⬦ Beads
- ⬦ Pins   ⬦ Buttons
- ⬦ Ribbon   ⬦ Stars
- ⬦ Glitter   ⬦ Yarn or string

Method:

Several techniques are suggested below. They can be used alone or several can be combined. Choose any or all of them to make a variety of pine cone decorations.

1. Glue or pin brightly colored ribbon to the base of the pine cone. Make a bow as a decoration and a loop to hang the ornament.

2. Dab glue on the edges of the pine cone and sprinkle glitter over it. Shake off the excess glitter before hanging the decoration.

3. Glue beads and buttons to the pine cone.

4. Trim the edges of a pine cone with red or green paint.

5. Decorate a pine cone with gold or silver stars.

Ornament hooks, clear fishline, ribbon, yarn, thread, or string can be used to hang the pine cone from the tree.

Yule Log

Burning the yule log is a very old Christmas custom associated with the French Canadian people. A huge length of wood, ceremoniously cut and brought into the house, is set aflame before the family leaves to attend the Christmas Eve mass. The yule log is said to have magical powers. If it sends out many sparks, the family will have a good year.

Since many of today's homes do not have fireplaces, the custom of burning the log has diminished. People still remember the tradition by making decorations and delicacies in the shape of a yule log. Below are directions for a decoration that can be used as a table centerpiece.

Materials:

- ✧ Round cardboard container
- ✧ Construction paper
   (brown, white, red, and green)
- ✧ Paper tube

- ✧ Scissors
- ✧ Glue
- ✧ Markers
- ✧ Masking or duct tape

Method:

Construct the yule log from a round cardboard container such as an empty oatmeal box. Cover the cylinder with brown paper. Using the end of the container as a pattern, draw two circles onto brown paper and cut them out. Glue one to each end of the log.

Cover a small tube, such as a bathroom tissue or paper towel roll, with white paper. Cut a flame from red paper and glue it to the inside of one end of the tube. Tape the completed candle to the center of the brown log.

Cut out green holly leaves and red berries from construction paper. Glue them to the front of the log.

Carols

"O Holy Night" is traditionally sung at the stroke of midnight on Christmas Eve. It was written by Adolphe Adam, a French composer whose works included music for grand opera, comic opera, and the ballet. Another favorite French carol is "Angels We Have Heard on High."

Story

"Christmas in Hidden Valley," found in the book *Christmas Stories 'Round the World* (Lois J. Johnson, Chicago: Rand McNally, 1970), is a short story about a Canadian boy's secret Christmas wish to learn how to write his name.

Culinary

A Christmas cake, called *buche de Noel*, is a holiday favorite in the shape of a yule log. The recipe for this special dessert, as well as for a traditional, crusty french bread are included here.

Buche de Noel

Thin yellow sponge cake is filled with chocolate butter cream, rolled into the shape of a log, and covered with more chocolate frosting. Running a fork over the icing creates the texture of bark. Often the dessert is decorated with sprigs of holly and berries.

Ingredients:

- ✧ 1 cup flour
- ✧ 1 teaspoon baking powder
- ✧ 1/4 teaspoon salt
- ✧ 3 eggs
- ✧ 1 cup sugar
- ✧ 1/4 cup water
- ✧ 1 tablespoon lemon juice
- ✧ Powdered sugar

- ✧ 3/4 cup powdered sugar
- ✧ 3 squares chocolate, melted and cooled
- ✧ 1 teaspoon salt
- ✧ 2 teaspoons instant coffee
- ✧ 1 teaspoon vanilla
- ✧ 3 egg whites
- ✧ 1 1/4 cups powdered sugar, sifted
- ✧ 1/2 cup margarine, softened

Method:

Sift together the flour, baking powder, and salt. Beat three eggs at high speed until they are thick and light. Add one cup sugar a few tablespoons at a time. Beat the mixture until it is very thick. Blend in water and lemon juice. Gently fold the dry ingredients into the egg mixture. Spread evenly on a ten inch by fifteen inch jelly roll pan that is lined with lightly greased waxed paper.

Bake the cake for twelve to fifteen minutes at 375 degrees until it springs back when lightly touched. Sprinkle a towel with powdered sugar and turn the cake onto it. Remove the waxed paper. Roll up the cake and towel from the short side. Cool on a rack.

To make the chocolate filling, cream together the softened margarine and powdered sugar. Melt and cool three squares of chocolate. Add to the butter and flour. Add salt, instant coffee, and vanilla. Beat the egg whites very stiff. Gradually add the sifted powdered sugar. Stir into the chocolate mixture.

Spread half of the filling on the jelly roll. Roll up the cake. Place remaining filling in a pastry tube with a star tip. Decorate the outside of the cake with strips of frosting to resemble a log. Garnish with nuts.

French Bread

Crusty french bread is found at almost every meal. The long slender loaf is called *baguette*.

Ingredients:

- ✦ 1 package active dry yeast
- ✦ 2 cups warm water
- ✦ 1 teaspoon salt
- ✦ 2 teaspoons sugar
- ✦ 5 - 6 cups white flour

Method:

Dissolve one package of yeast in two cups warm water. Add salt, sugar, and three cups of flour. Stir until smooth. Then add additional flour, usually two to three cups, until the dough is stiff. Knead on a floured board until smooth and elastic, about ten minutes. Let the dough rise in a bowl covered with a clean towel until it doubles in size. Punch down and shape into two long loaves. Place the loaves on a cookie sheet. Cut three to four diagonal slashes across the loaves. Cover with a towel and let it rise again until double in size. Sprinkle with water. Bake at 375 degrees for thirty-five to forty minutes. Sprinkle more water on top several times during baking to give the bread its chewy French crust. Serve warm.

Game

━━━━━━━━━━━■━━━━━━━━━━━

Review some of the French Canadian Christmas customs by playing a game of bingo.

Divide a piece of paper into twenty-five squares. Reproduce a sheet for each participant. Brainstorm a list of twenty-five words associated with the celebration of Christmas in the French speaking region of Canada. The list may include:

Noel	Crèche
Santon	*Le Reveillon*
Christmas rose	Pere Noel
Nativity	*Joyeux Noel*
Fresh flowers	Stained glass

Pine cones
Fruit stalls
Pastry shop (*Patisserie*)
Fish shop (*Poissonnerie*)
Candy shop (*Confiserie*)
Midnight worship service
Gifts
Music

Pâté
Butcher shop (*Boucherie*)
French bread
Cheeses
"O Holy Night"
Shoes
Yule log

Distribute a game card to each player. Read the list of twenty-five items, one at a time, and invite the group to write one custom in each square of their sheet. When the game cards have been prepared, call off each item in random order and tell the players to put an "X" in the square containing it or to cover the word with a marker, such as a button or a penny. The game is completed when one player has covered five squares in any direction, or when all players have made a bingo.

▪ECUADOR▪

Country Information

▪

*E*cuador, on South America's Pacific coast, is bounded on the north by Columbia and on the south and east by Peru. It is the fourth smallest republic in South America and covers about the same area as the state of Colorado.

Several ethnic groups comprise Ecuador's ten and a half million inhabitants. The population includes Indian (25%); Mestizo, a mixture of Indian and Spanish (55%); Spanish (10%); African (10%). The predominant religion is Roman Catholic.

Ecuador has four distinct topographical regions. The coastal plain is a rich agricultural belt where most of the country's tropical export crops are grown. Its waters are rich in shrimp, tuna, and other seafood. The highlands lie between two Andean mountain chains. The eastern region is covered with dense tropical forests and is the source of almost all of Ecuador's oil. The Galapagos Islands are located in the Pacific Ocean about six hundred miles off the coast.

Ecuador's natural resources include petroleum, fish, shrimp, timber, gold, and limestone. Bananas, coffee, cocoa, seafood, sugar, rice, corn, and livestock are the chief agricultural products. The primary industries are food processing, wood products, textiles, and chemicals.*

---

* Adams, Juanita, Editor. *Background Notes: Ecuador*. Washington, DC: United States Department of State, 1986.

Flag

The background of Ecuador's flag is made up of yellow, blue, and red horizontal bands. The colors are those of the Republic of Greater Colombia, of which Ecuador was a part until 1830. A coat of arms in the center is framed by a condor, the national bird, and lance-tipped banners.

Greetings

The official language of Ecuador is Spanish. Indian languages, especially Quechwa, are also recognized. The greeting of the season is *Feliz Navidad*. The greeting of peace is *paz*.

Customs

Many celebrations in Ecuador are centered around religious holidays. Preparations for Christmas, Easter, and saints' days are begun well in advance. For these occasions, unusual breads are baked and shared. In the spirit of an Ecuadorian festival, participate in a prayer service, "Blessing the Christmas Bread."

Materials:

- Bread, one loaf per family and one loaf to share
- Basket
- Table
- White tablecloth
- Candle
- Matches
- Music for selected songs
- Recorded music
- Tape, record, or CD player

Method:

Provide a variety of breads, one loaf per family, or invite each group to bring a loaf of their favorite bread to exchange.

Set up a table large enough to hold a basket and the bread. Use a white tablecloth and a candle. One loaf of bread to share among all the participants is also needed.

Call to Prayer

Leader: We gather in prayer in the presence of our God who shares divinity with us in the form of bread, who shares humanity with us through a manger birth, who fills us and inspires us through breath of the Spirit. Let us give praise and thanks!

All: Amen!

Song: "Child So Lovely" or another appropriate song

Scripture Reading

(adapted from Lk 1:26–32, Lk 2:1–40, Lk 3:23, Lk 4:1, and Lk 22:14–20)

The angel Gabriel was sent from God, to a virgin betrothed to a man named Joseph, of the house of David. The virgin's name was Mary.

Upon arriving, the angel said to her: "Rejoice, O highly favored daughter! The Lord is with you. You shall conceive and bear a son and give him the name Jesus. Great will be his love and he will be called the Bread of Life."

A decree was published ordering a census of the whole world. Joseph took Mary, his wife, who was with child, to the town of Bethlehem to be counted.

While they were there the days of her confinement were completed. She gave birth to her firstborn son and wrapped him in swaddling clothes and laid him in a manger.

There were shepherds living in the fields keeping night watch over their flocks. The angel of the Lord appeared to them and said: "You have nothing to fear! I come to proclaim good news to you — tidings of great joy to be shared by all people. This day a Savior has been born to you, the Messiah."

The shepherds went in haste and found Mary and Joseph. Once they saw the baby lying in the manger, they understood what had been told to them.

When the eighth day arrived for his circumcision, the name Jesus was given to the child, the name the angel had given him before he was conceived.

At that time there was a certain man named Simeon. He was a just man, and the Holy Spirit was upon him. He came to the temple, inspired by the Spirit. He took the child in his arms and said to Mary his mother: "This child is destined to be the downfall and the rise of many people, a sign that will be opposed — he shall be pierced with a sword — so that the thoughts of many hearts may be laid bare."

When all had been fulfilled, Mary and Joseph took the child and returned to their own town of Nazareth. The child grew in size and stature, filled with wisdom, and the grace of God was upon him.

When Jesus began his public ministry he was about thirty years of age. Full of the Holy Spirit, he began to teach in the synagogues and his reputation spread. He cured people's blindness, he opened the ears of the deaf, he healed lepers, and he called people to be his disciples and to follow him. He would teach in the temple by day, and leave the city to spend the night on the Mount of Olives.

On the night before his death, Jesus sat with his friends, those who had followed him. He took bread and gave thanks to God the Creator. He broke the bread and gave it to them, saying: "This is my body to be given for you. When you eat this, remember me always." They shared it among themselves and their hearts were filled with love.

Scripture Sharing

Invite those present to share their thoughts and feelings on the scripture reading. Focus in on what it means to be bread for each other.

Blessing

Leader: We ask you, Creator God, giver of all life, to bless this Christmas bread as we offer it to you and to one another. Let us offer this bread to each other with open hand and heart. Jesus was born in poverty and later became bread for our sharing. Bless us, Redeemer God, and bless all people who share bread and life.

All: Amen!

Ritual Action

At this time break the common loaf of bread and invite all those present to take and eat. After all have eaten of the one loaf a person from each household should come to the prayer table and receive a loaf of bread to take home and share as a family. Play soft Christmas music at this time.

Closing Ritual

Offer one another a sign of peace. Continue to play soft music.

Closing Prayer

Leader: We give you thanks, God of holy life, for bread shared, songs sung, friendships strengthened, and hope given. With these gifts we are fed and nourished. Because of this we are more able to be faithful. Continue to nourish, heal, and love us, that we might help make a more peaceful world.

All: Amen!

Closing Song: "Cold December Flies Away" or another appropriate song

Crèche

———————■———————

In the grandest hacienda or the most humble hut in Ecuador, the nativity scene, called a *pesebre*, holds a place of honor. Set in or near the entrance hallway of the home, the crèche becomes a family shrine. The figures, including burros and llamas, are generally made from bread dough. Often the scene is set up in a small box and a picture of Bethlehem painted on blue paper serves as the lining.

Create a crèche similar to one that might be found in an Ecuadorian home during the Christmas season. Each batch of bread dough will make about seven three-inch figures.

Materials:

- ◇ Shoe box
- ◇ White bread
- ◇ White glue
- ◇ Cold cream
- ◇ Paint, tempera or acrylic
- ◇ Brushes
- ◇ Mixing bowls or containers
- ◇ Water

Method:

Remove the crusts from twenty-four slices of bread. Crumble the bread into a bowl. Add twelve ounces of white glue. Before blending the bread and the glue, the person doing the mixing should rub his or her hands with cold cream. Combine the ingredients and knead the mixture until it's no longer sticky. Divide the dough into two equal balls.

One ball, uncolored, will be used to form the basic creche figures. Color will be added to the remaining dough, which will be used for details on the people and animals. Sub-divide the second ball into small pieces. One lump will be needed for each color required. Knead a drop of paint into each of the small balls.

Form the basic figures from the uncolored dough.

In another container, mix water and white glue in equal parts. Brush this mixture onto one of the creche figures. Add details such as hair, eyes, clothing, belt and flowers to the figure by making rolls, coils and tiny balls with the colored dough. Press the features onto the figure and brush the entire finished character with the white glue mixture. Allow the piece to dry.

Continue this process until the desired number of people and animals are constructed.

Paint the inside and outside of a shoe box with tempera paint and decorate it to resemble the town of Bethlehem. Glue pieces of colored dough to the box with white glue to make three-dimensional decorations in the background. Set or glue the figures into the box.

Set the scene in a prominent place in the home, classroom, or church and enjoy it during the Christmas season.

Gift Giver

Papa Noel, much like the North American Santa Claus, dresses in a long red coat and brings good cheer to all people. Christmas is a very religious feast day, and the true gift giver is the Christ Child. It is thought that the infant Jesus visits the children during the night and leaves special gifts for the girls and boys.

Epiphany, January 6, is the time when gift exchanges take place. Presents are delivered by the Magi during the feast of the three kings.

Card

Molas are layers of colored materials such as paper or cloth. This Ecuadorian folk art has been inspired by the Indian people. Try making a paper *mola* and use it to create a Christmas card.

Materials:

- Construction paper, four colors
- Construction paper, white
- Scissors
- Ruler
- Scrap paper
- Pencil
- Glue
- Crayons or markers
- Small scrap pieces of cardboard

Method:

Select four different colors of construction paper to use for the *mola*. Measure and cut each sheet to a 4" x 5" rectangle. Place the four sheets on top of each other and cut a tiny notch on each side. The notches will keep the sheets lined up during the cutting and construction process.

On a piece of scrap paper, use a pencil and draw a design for the card. Use a simple, bold shape, such as a flower, manger, or sun. Color the symbol with three of the four colors that will be used for the *mola*.

On the sheet of construction paper in the fourth color, lightly draw the symbol. Cut all the parts of the design from this paper. This piece will be the top sheet of the *mola*.

Place the cut sheet of paper over the piece of construction paper that is the most dominant color of the design. Cut out from the second sheet all of the design parts except those that are the same color as this piece of paper.

Place the second sheet of paper over the piece of construction paper that is the second most dominant color in the design. Cut out from this third sheet all the design parts except the parts that are the same color as the sheet being cut.

Put the three cut sheets over the fourth sheet, but do no cutting on the fourth sheet.

The four sheets of construction paper are now ready to be assembled. Small pieces of cardboard will be placed between them to add to the design and texture of the *mola*. Glue the sheets together starting with the bottom uncut piece. Place the next sheet on top of it. Set several tiny pieces of cardboard between the two sheets so that the second one is a fraction of an inch above the first. Glue the pieces of cardboard to the bottom sheet of paper. Matching notches, glue the second piece on top of the cardboard bits, making sure that none of the cardboard pieces show through.

Glue the third sheet of paper to the first in the same way. Do the same with the last piece. The paper *mola* design is now completed.

Fold the white sheet of construction paper in half to make a card. Glue the *mola* design to the front of it. Write a greeting on the inside and give it as a special Christmas gift.*

Crafts

—■—

Ecuadorian people are well known for their skill as artisans. Detailed pottery, bold jewelry, beautiful tinwork, and intricate weavings are some of the most famous arts and crafts of the country. These objects provide useful and necessary items and often supply additional income. Directions for a weaving decoration and a tinwork project are offered. Use these techniques to make Christmas decorations, tree ornaments, or special gifts.

---

*Shoemaker, Kathryn. *Creative Christmas: Simple Crafts From Many Lands*. Minneapolis: Winston Press, 1978.

Decorative Weaving

Textiles of the Otavalo Indians are well known for their distinctive weave, bright colors, and depictions of the Ecuadorian landscape. Try making a weaving and using it as a decoration.

Materials:

- ◇ Dowel rods
- ◇ Burlap, dark green, two-thirds of a yard
- ◇ Yarn (medium weight), bright pink and bright orange, one skein each
- ◇ Yarn (heavy), lime green, five skeins
- ◇ Needle
- ◇ Thread (heavy)
- ◇ Saw
- ◇ Scissors
- ◇ Sewing machine
- ◇ Plastic ring

Method:

Cut the dowels to the following dimensions: 1 - 24"; 2 - 18"; 2 - 9".

Cut the burlap to the shape shown in the diagram. With a machine, sew the illustrated areas with a zig-zag stitch to secure them. Pull the threads from the remaining area as the diagram shows. Gather six to eight strands of burlap in each of the pulled areas and tie them in the center with a piece of yarn or thread.

Attach loops of rug yarn to the dowel rods so that the loops hang down five inches. Glue the ends in place. Secure the five dowels firmly to the top edge of each solid strip of burlap by stitching over them with heavy green thread or yarn.

Form a tab for the top of the hanging from a piece of green burlap or felt. Sew securely to the top of the piece.

Create pink and orange pompons by winding yarn around a piece of heavy cardboard. The large pompons should be made on a 2 1/2" piece, and the smaller ones on a 1 1/2" piece. Tie the yarn securely in the center and cut it at the bottom and the top. Trim to make a fluffy ball. Make ten of each color and sew them to various places on the hanging. Attach a plastic curtain ring to the top of the center of the tab to hang the decoration from the ceiling.*

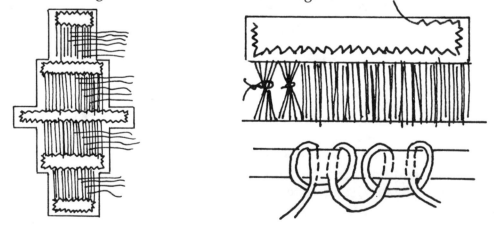

---

* Erickson, Joyce. *In Straw and Story: Christmas Resources for Home and Church.* Elgin, IL: Brethren Press, 1983, p. 147.

Tin Ornaments

Make simple tin decorations from heavy foil wrap or aluminum pie plates and TV dinner trays and use them as ornaments.

Materials:

- ✧ Aluminum pie plates
- ✧ Scissors
- ✧ Thread
- ✧ Permanent markers
- ✧ Paper
- ✧ Pencil
- ✧ Yarn

Method:

Think of symbols associated with the celebration of the twelve days of Christmas in Ecuador. Draw a simple shape on paper and cut it out. Using the cut-out as a pattern, place it on foil or aluminum and trace around it with a permanent marker. Cut out the design. Decorate it in various colors with permanent marker. Poke a small hole in the top of the metal. Thread with yarn for hanging. Use the tin piece as an ornament. Make several additional shapes.

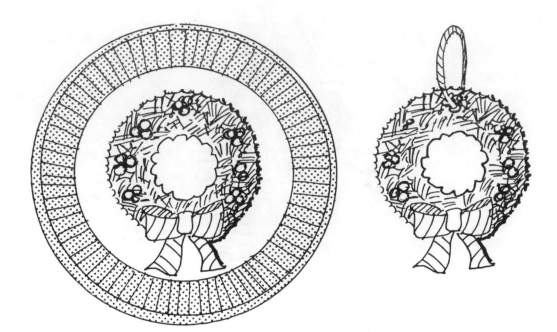

Carols

—————■—————

Many Christmas carols have been written in Spanish. *The International Book of Christmas Carols* (Ehret, Walter and George K. Evans, Battleboro, VT: Stephen Greene Press, 1980) includes twenty-seven of them. Seasonal songs, with both English and Spanish texts, are printed in many revised hymnals.

Two carols you might want to look for are: "Child So Lovely" (Nino Lindo) and "Cold December Flies Away" (En el Frio Invernal).

Story

—————■—————

The rich customs and the many stories that belong to the people of Ecuador enhance the celebrations in this country. For the Ecuadorians, Christmas is a day of religious celebrations. Children often dress in costumes, generally as saints, and go door to door asking their neighbors for blessings.

January 6, Epiphany, is the day of gift giving in Ecuador. It is often called Children's Day. Gifts are given, holiday songs are sung, and parties are held on the feast of the three kings.

Tell the story of the Magi's visit. Proclaim it from scripture (Matthew 2), recite it from memory, or use the paraphrase provided.

Set up a small table for the storytelling. Place symbols of the gifts brought by the three kings on it. Play soft background music, light a candle, and tell the story.

The Visit of the Magi

Long ago, three kings lived in cities far from each other: Melchior of Arabia, Gaspar of Tharsis, and Balthasar of Saba. The three kings were astrologers. They watched the stars day and night from their eastern lands. They knew what stars rose at certain times of the year and what stars to look for in the sky.

One night a glorious new star appeared in the sky, a star that the kings had not seen before. They consulted their books and learned that this special star was a sign that a king was to be born, a king for all people.

Each left his own country, and set out to follow the star and find the infant king. Each carried with him a gift. After days and nights of travel, the kings met and discovered they were following the same star. Together they continued.

As they came to Jerusalem they visited King Herod and asked, "Where is the newborn king? We have seen his star in far-off eastern lands, and have come to worship him."

King Herod, who was evil, was disturbed by this news. He consulted his elders and the people who knew the law. "The child king is to be born at Bethlehem in Judea," they replied, "for that is what the prophet Micah wrote." King Herod then informed the travelers, "Go and make a careful search for the infant king in Bethlehem, then report back to me so that I too may go and honor him."

The three kings set off for Bethlehem to find the newborn king. Once again they followed the wondrous star until it rested above the place where the child had been born. Going into the place they saw the child with his mother Mary, and they bowed down to worship him. Then they opened their treasures and gave him gifts of gold and of incense and of myrrh. Because God warned them in a dream not to go back to Herod, they returned home by another way.

Culinary

━━━━━━━■━━━━━━━

Since Christmas is celebrated during the summer in Ecuador, ripe fruits are in abundance. Christmas dinner may feature roast lamb, baked potatos, and brown sugar bread. Recipes for two special treats, *Bunuelos* and *Almond Empanaditas*, are provided.

Bunuelos

Bunuelos, puffy anise flavored doughnuts, are served on December 17, the day honoring the Virgin of Solitude, and throughout the Advent and Christmas seasons.

Ingredients:

- ✧ 4 tablespoons butter
- ✧ 3/4 cup milk
- ✧ 1 tablespoon anise seed
- ✧ 2 eggs, beaten
- ✧ 3 cups flour
- ✧ 1 teaspoon baking powder
- ✧ 1 teaspoon salt
- ✧ Cooking oil
- ✧ 1/2 cup sugar
- ✧ 1 teaspoon ground cinnamon

Method:

Heat the butter, milk, and anise seed in a saucepan until boiling. Cool. Stir in two beaten eggs. Sift the flour, baking powder, and salt together. Add the egg mixture to the dry ingredients and knead the dough on a lightly floured board until smooth. Shape the dough into twenty little balls. Let it rest for five minutes. Roll each ball into a four inch circle. Fry in deep fat (375 degrees) for four minutes, turning once. Drain on paper towels.

Combine the sugar and cinnamon in a paper bag. Shake the doughnuts in the sugar mixture.

Makes twenty bunuelos.

Almond Empanaditas

Ingredients:

- ✧ 2 cups sifted all purpose flour
- ✧ 1 teaspoon salt
- ✧ 2 teaspoons baking powder
- ✧ 1/2 cup shortening
- ✧ 1/2 to 2/3 cup ice water

- ✧ 3/4 cup blanched almonds, chopped
- ✧ 1/2 cup sugar
- ✧ 1 teaspoon ground cinnamon
- ✧ 1 egg white
- ✧ 1 teaspoon almond extract

Method:

Sift flour, salt, and baking powder together. Cut in shortening until the mixture resembles coarse crumbs. Add ice water one tablespoon at a time until all the flour is moistened. Shape into a ball. Roll out on lightly floured surface until it is 1/8 inch thick. Cut into 2 1/2 inch circles. Mix together almonds, sugar, and cinnamon. Beat egg white and extract until frothy. Stir in almond mixture. Place one teaspoon of almond filling on half of each circle of dough. Wet the edges, fold over and seal the edges with the tines of a fork. Fry in hot oil, 375 degrees, about four minutes or until golden brown, turning once. Drain on paper toweling. Makes three dozen.

Game

The crossword puzzle below uses words that refer to the many things you've discovered about Ecuador, its people, and its celebration of the season of Christmas.

Clues:

ACROSS

1. Burned during worship (Incense)
2. Official language (Spanish)
3. Peace (*Paz*)
4. Christmas Gift Giver (Papa Noel)
5. Food (Rice)

DOWN

1. Ethnic group (Indian)
2. January 6 (Epiphany)
3. Sweet Crop (Sugar)
4. Three Kings (Magi)
5. Gift (Gold)

6. National bird (Condor)
7. Mixture of Indian
   and Spanish (Mestizo)

6. Religion (Catholic)
7. Offering (Myrrh)
8. Shellfish (Shrimp)

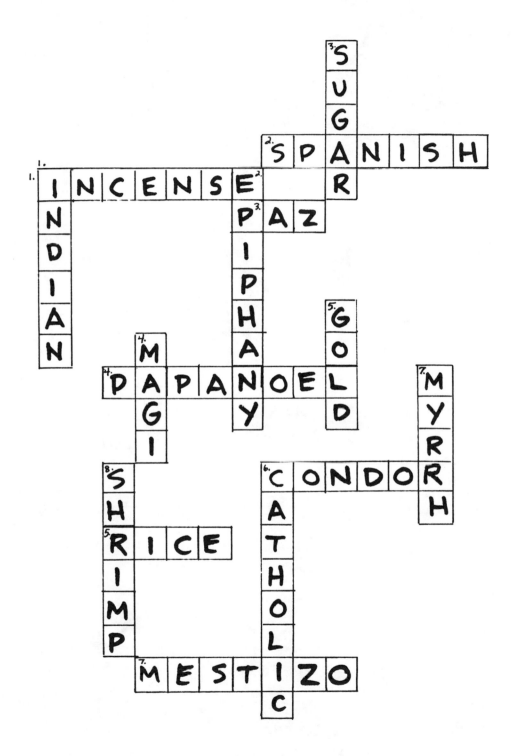

▪GERMANY▪

Country Information

▪

Germany, located in north central Europe, is bordered by the North Sea and the Baltic Sea and is surrounded by Denmark, the Netherlands, Belgium, Luxembourg, France, Switzerland, Austria, Czechoslovakia, and Poland. The terrain varies from low plains in the north, high plains, hills, and basins in the center, and mountainous Alpine regions in the south.

For nearly forty years following World War II the country was politically divided into West Germany and East Germany, two German states in one German nation physically split by a 103-mile wall. Since reunification in 1990, the population of Germany totals seventy-eight and a half million people. The inhabitants are primarily German. Approximately half of the population is Roman Catholic and half is Protestant.

Germany has produced some of the world's greatest composers, artists, writers, scholars, and scientists.

Natural resources include iron, hard coal, lignite, potash, and natural gas. Major agricultural products are corn, wheat, potatoes, sugar beets, barley, and hops. This region is also known for its viniculture, forestry, and fisheries. Iron and steel, coal, chemicals, electrical products, ships, vehicles, and construction are primary industries.*

---

* Holly, Susan, Editor. *Background Notes: Germany.* Washington, DC: United States Department of State, 1991.

Flag

Three horizontal bands — black, red, and gold (from top to bottom) — form the field of the German flag.

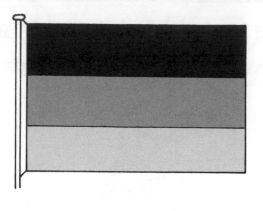

Greetings

The Christmas greeting in German is *Froehliche Weinachten*. The word for peace is *Frieden*.

Customs

Holiday celebrations in Germany begin on the first Sunday in Advent (late November or early December) and continue through Epiphany, January 6. Germany has introduced many customs that are now observed throughout the world. Among these are the Advent calendar, Advent wreath, and Christmas tree.

Children use Advent calendars to count the number of days from the beginning of the season until Christmas. A small numbered window, opened each day, reveals a picture of something associated with the season. The last square is opened on Christmas Day.

The Advent wreath, a circle of greenery with four candles, may be hung from the ceiling or set on a table. One candle is lit on each of the four Sundays of Advent until all four are brightly ablaze. The family gathers around the wreath each evening before or after dinner, sings a hymn, and lights the appropriate number of candles for the week.

Early in December, many German cities feature Christmas fairs, or markets, called *Christkindlesmarkets*. At these huge outdoor events shoppers can purchase wooden and mechanical toys, glass ornaments, gingerbread figures, and marzipan candies. Christmas carolers and bands add to the festivities.

Saint Nicholas Day is observed on December 6 and a kindly old man, dressed in bishop's garb, delivers small gifts and goodies to good girls and boys throughout the land.

Many legends are associated with the origin of the Christmas tree. Some say that

Saint Boniface, an English missionary who brought Christianity to Germany around 720, was the first to use the evergreen tree as a symbol of Christ. The most famous story involves Martin Luther, a leader of the Reformation. While walking home from church one clear starry night, he was inspired by the beauty of the scene and wanted to share it with his family. He cut down a small evergreen tree, brought it home, and decorated it with tiny candles. The candles symbolized Christ, the light of the world, and the evergreen tree represented the eternal life Jesus offers to believers.

Today the tradition of the tree continues to be a source of enchantment and excitement for young and old alike. The tree is placed in a special room that is guarded and sometimes even locked until time for viewing. Parents trim the tree with shiny tinsel, brightly colored ornaments, cookies baked into a variety of shapes, and small candles. On Christmas Eve the doors to the room are opened, the candles lighted, and the entire household gathers around the tree to sing favorite songs such as "Silent Night" and "O Tannenbaum." In many households small tables, one for each family member, surround the tree and are filled with gifts left by Christkindl. Handmade presents are still a special tradition.

Attendance at church services is an important practice in German families. Christmas Eve festivities include a midnight service. Customarily, all church bells peal at midnight. Services are always held on Christmas morning and often on December 26, the second day of Christmas.

Christmas festivities continue through Epiphany, January 6. Traditionally on that day a man appears in the street as soon as it is dark carrying a lantern in the shape of a star set on top of a tall pole. The children of the village follow behind him. Each person carries a lighted star and many wear crowns and costumes. Called the Star Singers, the children process through town caroling.

On the night of Epiphany the candles on the Christmas tree are lighted for the last time. The tree is then discarded, signaling that the celebration of Christmas has been completed.

Crèche

German families decorate their trees with figures and symbols shaped with cookie dough. Shapes include Saint Nicholas, hearts, stars, and figures and animals from the nativity story. In this tradition, create a cookie dough crèche. Use cookie cutters to make the shapes, or find pictures of the central figures in coloring books or magazines and use them to make patterns. Hang the pieces on the tree and share them with family and friends during and after the holiday season.

Two variations on a sugar cookie recipe are provided.

Ornament Cookies

Ingredients:

- ✧ 1/3 cup shortening
- ✧ 1/3 cup sugar
- ✧ 1 teaspoon soda
- ✧ 1 teaspoon salt

- ◇ 1 egg
- ◇ 2/3 cup honey
- ◇ 1 teaspoon lemon flavoring
- ◇ 2 3/4 cups flour
- ◇ Cookie cutters
- ◇ Frosting
- ◇ Decorations
- ◇ Ribbon

Method:

Mix shortening, sugar, egg, honey, and flavoring thoroughly. Stir together flour, soda, and salt and blend into the shortening mixture. Chill dough. Heat oven to 375 degrees. Roll dough 1/4 inch thick. Cut into desired shapes. Poke a hole into the top of each cookie to string ribbon through later. Place one inch apart on lightly greased baking sheet. Bake eight to ten minutes. When cool, ice and decorate as desired. Thread a piece of ribbon through the hole in the top of each cookie to hang it on the tree.

For molasses cookies, substitute brown sugar for granulated sugar, molasses for honey, two teaspoons cinnamon and one teaspoon ginger for lemon flavoring.

Gift Giver

German children receive presents from two gift givers during the holiday season. The first is Saint Nicholas, and young people anticipate his arrival by filling their shoes with hay for his horse before they go to bed on December 5. During the night Saint Nicholas, dressed in bishop's garb, rides his white horse and makes the rounds of the houses. Together with his companion Ruprecht, who is dressed in black, the pair leave cookies, candies, fruits, nuts, and small toys for good girls and boys.

Christkindl, the second gift giver, comes on Christmas Eve. It is believed that this angelic figure, with white robes, a golden crown, and large golden wings, is sent by the Christ Child to deliver gifts. Before the holiday, children write letters to the Christ Child to suggest the gifts that they would like to receive. To make sure that the letters will be seen they glue sugar on the envelope to serve as glitter and place the papers on the windowsill before going to bed. Doors or windows left slightly ajar on Christmas Eve allow Christkindl access to homes to distribute cookies, candies, toys, and bundles of knitted mittens, caps, and scarves.

In some areas it is believed that the Christ Child sends *Weihnachtsmann*, or Christmas man, to deliver gifts.

Card

Cards in the form of Advent calendars are sent at the beginning of December in Germany. Adapt this wonderful German tradition and use it to count the twelve days of Christmas.

Materials:

- ✧ Construction paper
- ✧ Scissors
- ✧ Colored pencils or markers
- ✧ Stickers, Christmas cards, or magazines
- ✧ Glue

Method:

Find a word or picture associated with the holiday celebration in Germany for each of the twelve days of Christmas. Below are some suggestions for categories.

✧ Flag	✧ Greeting of the season
✧ Greeting of peace	✧ Custom
✧ Crèche	✧ Gift giver
✧ Card	✧ Craft
✧ Carol	✧ Story
✧ Game	✧ Food

Follow the pattern on page 76 and prepare the two pieces for the card. The top sheet contains the numbered windows and the bottom sheet holds the illustrations. Choose a color of construction paper to use as the base of the card and glue or draw the twelve illustrations onto it. Be sure they are positioned in the order in which they are to be opened. Prepare the top sheet by drawing the windows and numbering them from one to twelve. Carefully slit each window on three sides.

Position the sheet with the windows over the sheet with the illustrations. Place glue in each corner and stick the two sheets together.

On Christmas Day, open window number one. Continue opening one window on each of the remaining eleven days of the season.

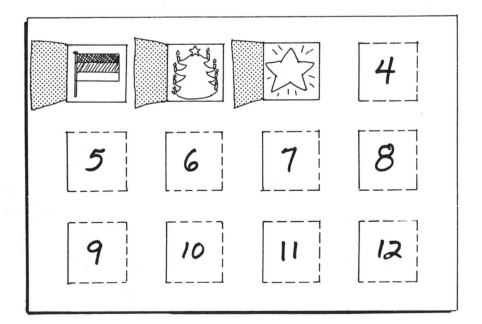

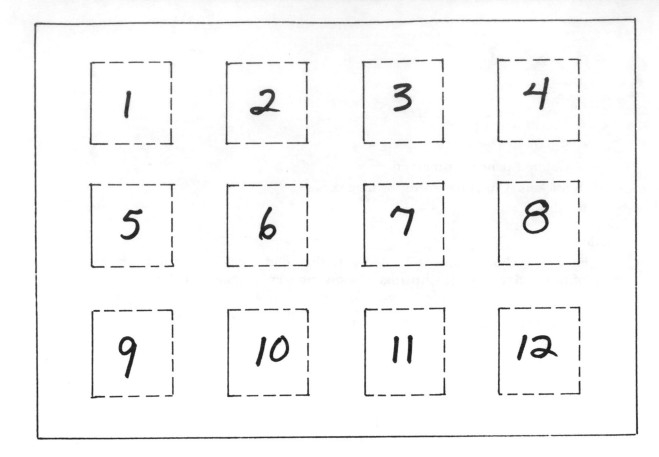

Crafts

■

Handmade candles are popular decorations in German homes and churches throughout the year and especially during the holiday season. For many centuries German artisans have designed candles with intricate patterns and reliefs, many of which were adapted from medieval woodcuts. Try carving a candle with a symbol or scene that is suitable for the Christmas season.

Germany is credited with introducing the use of the evergreen tree to the celebration of Christmas. Today decorated trees are used all over the world during the holiday season. Construct a three-dimensional paper Christmas tree to use as a decoration.

Christmas Candles

Materials:

◇ Candle (thick)   ◇ X-acto knife

◇ Pencil   ◇ Acrylic paint

◇ Paper   ◇ Brush

◇ Needle   ◇ Paper towel

Method:

Choose a candle that is quite thick and proportionately short. It should be a solid color.

Plan and practice the design for the candle by sketching it on a piece of paper. Attempt a Christmas tree, bell, or church, or choose from many other options. When the plan is satisfactory, use a needle and scratch the pattern lightly into the wax to serve as a guide. Carve the design into the candle with an X-acto knife or a similar precision blade.

Give the candle an antique appearance by covering the carved areas with a coat of acrylic paint. Use a color of paint that is darker than the candle. Brush a small amount of paint into the recesses of the carving and wipe it away with a paper towel. Allow the paint to dry.

Display the candle as a holiday decoration.

Three-Dimensional Christmas Tree

Materials:

- ✧ Posterboard or construction paper, green
- ✧ Scissors
- ✧ Hole punch
- ✧ Yarn or ribbon
- ✧ Stickers, stars, sequins

Method:

For each ornament, cut two evergreen shapes, using the pattern provided on page 79. Cut along the center line of each paper. Insert the tree with the slit at the top into the cut at the bottom of the other piece.

Decorate the tree with ornaments made from self-adhesive stickers, gummed stars, and other trims. Punch a hole in the top of the decoration with a paper punch. Attach a loop of ribbon or yarn through the hole to hang the ornament on the tree.

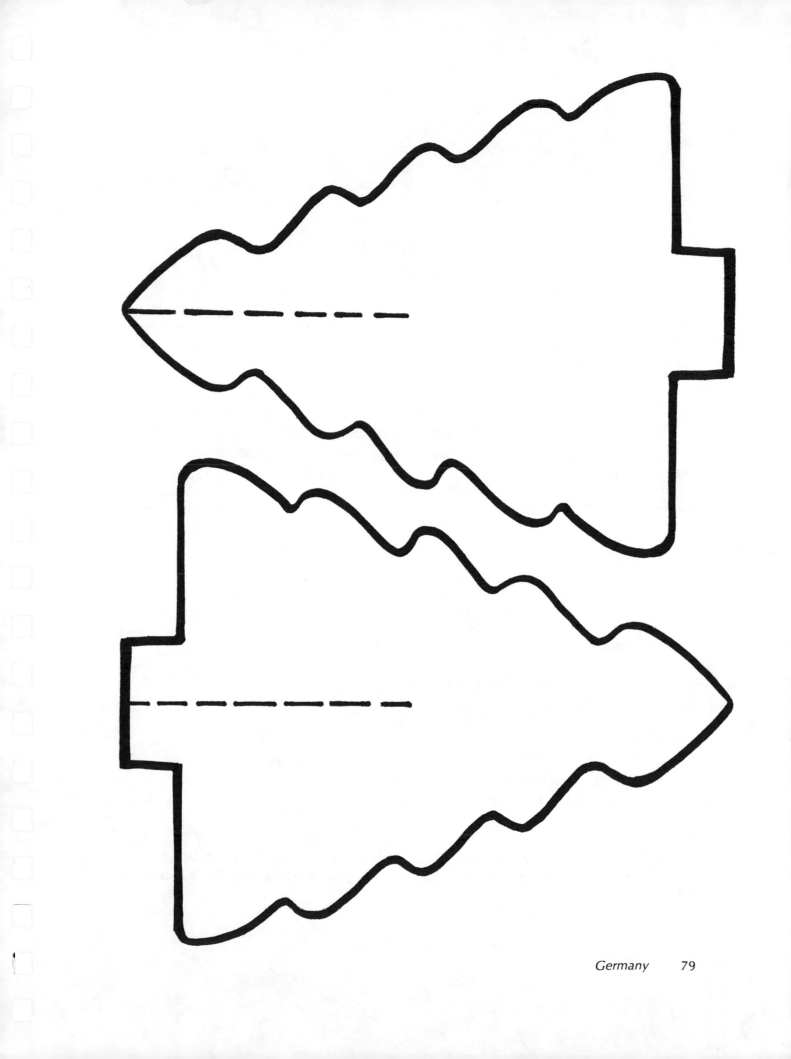

Carols

After German families attend Christmas Eve church services, they return home to an evening of festivities. The parents light the candles on the tree and the entire household gathers around it to sing carols of the season. Two German carols are "From Heaven Above I Come to You" and "Lo, How a Rose E'er Blooming."

Story

The Shoemaker and the Elves (The Brothers Grimm. Illustrated by Adrienne Adams. New York: Charles Scribner's Sons, 1960) is a familiar German folktale of a poor shoemaker and his wife who find beautifully made new shoes on their workbench every morning. The grateful couple lovingly repay the Christmas elves with a gift of handmade clothing.

Culinary

During Advent, German families get ready to celebrate Christmas in many ways. Preparing and purchasing special foods is one of them. Activity and aroma fill the kitchen as traditional breads and cookies are baked. These will be shared with family and friends during the holidays. Energy and effort may also be spent constructing and decorating gingerbread houses to serve as decoration and dessert.

Various types of candies, cookies, and other culinary favorites fill the booths at the outdoor Christmas markets and line the windows of local bake shops. Marzipan candy formed into the shapes of fruits, vegetables, and animals are among the special treats, as are huge pretzels. Recipes are included for marzipan and pretzels.

Christmas Eve dinner may feature a main course of fish, while the noon meal after church on December 25 is often roasted stuffed goose. Customarily each child receives a marzipan candy pig as part of the dessert course.

Marzipan Candy

Ingredients:

- ⬥ 8 ounces almond paste
- ⬥ 2/3 cup marshmallow creme
- ⬥ 2 tablespoons light corn syrup
- ⬥ 1/2 cup powdered sugar
- ⬥ Food coloring

Method:

Blend all ingredients together. Knead well and form into shapes of different fruits, vegetables, and little animals. Brush with food coloring. Coloring may also be mixed into the dough.

Giant Pretzels

Ingredients:

- ✧ 1 package yeast
- ✧ 1 1/2 cups warm water (105 to 115 degrees)
- ✧ 1/2 teaspoon sugar
- ✧ 4 1/2 cups flour
- ✧ 1 egg yolk
- ✧ 2 tablespoons water
- ✧ Coarse salt

Method:

Dissolve the yeast in the warm water and add the sugar. Stir in the flour and knead for six minutes. Let the dough rise, covered, in a greased bowl until double in size. Divide the dough into twelve pieces and roll them into long sticks. Blend together the egg yolk and water and brush small amounts of the liquid on the pretzel sticks. Sprinkle coarse salt over the dough.

Bake the pretzels for twelve minutes at 450 degrees. Makes twelve giant pretzels.

Game

━━━━━━━━━━■━━━━━━━━━━

Unscramble the word(s) on each line and form an acrostic that describes the many components of a German Christmas.

A	ANVDTE LRADENAC
G	GEBGIENRDAR SOHEU
E	HYPNAPIE
R	SILEGIOUR CSERESVI
M	IRZNAMPA YACDN
A	DETAVN REHAWT
N	LISANCOH
C	DRILHISNCTK
H	MNAHDEDA SIFGT
R	PHTURECR
I	LISEICC
S	NSOSG
T	NBUNMTANAE
M	TRAMIN HUELRT
A	CIVESAIITT
S	TRSA NSGREIS

Below is the answer key for the word scramble that appears on the following page. The first letter of each word unscrambled makes up the phrase "A German Christmas."

A	A N V D T E L R A D E N A C	(ADVENT CALENDAR)
G	G E B G I E N R D A R S O H E U	(GINGERBREAD HOUSE)
E	H Y P N A P I E	(EPIPHANY)
R	S I L E G I O U R C S E R E S V I	(RELIGIOUS SERVICES)
M	I R Z N A M P A Y A C D N	(MARZIPAN CANDY)
A	D E T A V N R E H A W T	(ADVENT WREATH)
N	L I S A N C O H	(NICHOLAS)
C	D R I L H I S N C T K	(CHRISTKINDL)
H	M N A H D E D A S I F G T	(HANDMADE GIFTS)
R	P H T U R E C R	(RUPRECHT)
I	L I S E I C C	(ICICLES)
S	N S O S G	(SONGS)
T	N B U N M T A N A E	(TANNENBAUM)
M	T R A M I N H U E L R T	(MARTIN LUTHER)
A	C I V E S A I I T T	(ACTIVITIES)
S	T R S A N S G R E I S	(STAR SINGERS)

▪INDIA▪

Country Information

═══════════════════ ▪ ═══════════════════

*T*he Republic of India covers an area one-third the size of the United States. It shares common borders with Bangladesh, Burma, Pakistan, China, Tibet, Nepal, and Bhuton. India has three main terrains. Some of the highest mountains in the world, the Himalayas, extend along much of the northern border. A fertile, well-watered plain lies across a section of northern India. Hilly, plateau regions cover most of the rest of the area. The climate varies from tropical in the south to temperate in the north, with three distinct seasons throughout most of the country: cool, dry and hot, hot and rainy.

Eight hundred fifty million people inhabit India. Although the country occupies only 2.4 percent of the world's land area, it supports nearly fifteen percent of the world's population. Eighty-three percent of the people are Hindu, eleven percent are Muslim, and other religions include Christian, Sikh, Jain, Buddhist, and Parsi. Sixteen officially recognized languages are spoken in India; Hindi is the most widely spoken.

India has made considerable economic progress since its independence in 1947. A relatively sophisticated industrial base and a large pool of skilled labor have been created. Agriculture remains the crucial sector since it is influenced by the monsoons. Agricultural products include wheat, rice, coarse grains, oil seeds, sugar, and cotton.

Cotton and jute textile production continues to be the most important industry, but output in steel, machine tools, electric and transport machinery and chemicals has become more important in recent years. Natural resources include coal, iron ore, manganese, mica, bauxite, chromite, limestone, and barite.*

Flag

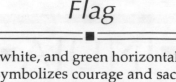

On India's flag, saffron, white, and green horizontal bands contain a blue spoked wheel in the center. Saffron symbolizes courage and sacrifice; white, peace and truth; green, faith and chivalry; and the spoked wheel, India's ancient culture.

Greetings

Hindi is spoken throughout India, although English is also recognized as a result of the long British presence in the country. The greeting of the season is *Merry Christmas*. The greeting of peace is the Hindi *Shanti*.

Customs

India is a land of diverse races, languages, and religious beliefs. Among the Hindus, Moslems, Buddhists, Sikhs, and Jews, Christians comprise approximately two percent of the population. Yet, during the season of Christmas, the birth of Christ is proclaimed joyously in homes, schools, and churches.

Preparations for the holiday begin long before December 25. Homes and churches are thoroughly cleaned. Dirt floors are replastered, walls are whitewashed, and brass is shined. Decorations include the poinsettia plant, which grows wild in India in the form of large bushes. Its green leaves turn bright scarlet during the Christmas season. Chains and tissue paper bells, used during the Indian celebration of *Diwali* in late October or early November, remain up in market stalls and shops during December and add to the festive atmosphere.

Early in December Christians in some areas of the country gather to raise the

---

* Lorfano, Paula M., Editor. *Background Notes: India*. Washington, DC: United States Department of State, 1989.

Christmas flag. This white banner with a red cross in the center is hoisted on a bamboo pole to serve as a reminder of the real meaning of Christmas. The cross stands as a symbol that the child of Christmas was born to become the Savior of the world.

On Christmas Eve, long, jubilant church services begin at midnight and last up to three hours. These times of worship provide an opportunity for Indian Christians to invite non-Christian friends and neighbors to hear the gospel story. Generally the scripture is presented through pageants and music programs.

Even though it is the middle of the night, parties take place after the service. Refreshments may include tea and cookies. Abraham cake, mounded rice covered with brown sugar, and barfi, a type of vanilla fudge covered with thin silver paper, are two traditional holiday treats.

The roofs of Christian homes are lined with little candles. These are lighted at Christmas and shine as a symbol of the birth of Jesus, the light of the world.

Christmas gifts are exchanged. Children receive one or two presents, generally an item for school and an article of clothing. Women may be given a shawl and men a blanket or scarf. New clothes for all family members are traditional once a year, and are received during the holiday season. In certain regions, lemons are given as symbols of good fortune and long life.

Crèche

The gospel story of the nativity is usually dramatized rather than read. A series of pantomimes depict the scenes. Present a series of tableaus (still life pictures) that portray the events.

Materials:

✧ Bible   ✧ Fabric pieces or costumes

Method:

Read the Christmas story from Luke 2. Decide which events will be portrayed. For example, the tableaus could include scenes of Mary and Joseph traveling to Bethlehem, the innkeeper telling the couple there is no room, the holy family in the stable, the angels appearing to the shepherds, and the shepherds visiting the newborn baby.

Invite people to participate in the various groups. Obtain costumes or use fabric pieces and drape them to suggest costumes. All participants should work together to pose a still scene. Several scenes in sequence may become a play. Present the Christmas story for a program or pageant using this form of drama.

Gift Giver

Since only a small percentage of India's population is Christian, the celebration of Christmas centers in homes, mission schools, hospitals, and churches. Christians proclaim the good news and share God's love in many ways.

Special visits are made to hospital patients, especially those in institutions sponsored by Christian organizations. They are given a holiday gift with religious significance. Often it will be a card with a picture and story of the birth of Jesus. This story culminates in the greatest gift of all, God's Son, Jesus, who was sent at Christmas to be the Savior of the world.

Card

Batik is a method of layering wax and dyes to create beautiful works of art. Originally batiks were used as head coverings, shawls, and wrap-around skirts worn by both women and men.

Directions are provided below for a simplified version of this technique. You can use it to depict a scene from Christmas celebrations in India, for example, a candle, a poinsettia, a manger, or a Madonna and Child. Attach the finished batik to the front of a folded piece of paper and give it as a unique greeting card.

Materials:

- Muslin, 100% cotton
- Pencil
- Ruler
- Permanent markers or fabric paints in various colors
- Meltex beeswax
- Paraffin
- Coffee can for heating waxes
- Paint brushes
- Wide container for dye
- Dye
- Water

- Brown paper bags
- Scissors
- Iron
- Pan or tray for hot iron
- Hot plate or electric skillet with temperature controls
- Newspaper
- Clothesline or cord
- Clip clothespins
- Fabric glue
- Paper
- Pen

Method:

Choose a piece of paper to use for the card and fold it in half. Be sure it is large enough so the batik print will show up well. Cut a piece of fabric slightly smaller than the front of the card. Cotton cloth such as muslin or old sheeting is excellent for batiks. New cloth should be washed and ironed before using it for the project. Avoid permanent press materials as they do not absorb the dyes well.

Decide on a design to use for the card and prepare a symbol for it. Use a pencil to sketch the design onto the material. With permanent markers or fabric paints, color the entire drawing.

Mix half Meltex beewax and half paraffin in a coffee can, and heat it on a hot plate or in an electric skillet. Controlling the heat is easier when using an electric skillet with various temperature settings. Be extremely careful to use low heat as wax is flammable at high temperatures.

Use a brush to paint the wax mixture over the entire surface of the design. Allow the wax to harden. Wrinkle the piece into a ball until the wax begins to crack slightly, then carefully open the cloth.

Gently slide the cloth into a wide container of a cold water dye bath or a warm tap water dye bath. Avoid dye solutions requiring boiling water; these will cause the wax to melt. Totally saturate the cloth with dye. Allow the piece to remain in the solution until it is a shade darker than desired as the cloth will lighten when it dries. Remove the fabric, blot it between newspaper, and clip it to the clothesline to air dry. Do not wring the cloth. Newspaper should cover the floor in this area.

When the cloth is dry place it between sheets of brown paper or split grocery bags. Old newspapers may also be used, provided they are at least a week old. Newer papers may transfer ink to the cloth. Iron the paper with a warm iron until the wax on the cloth is absorbed into the paper. Remove the brown paper.

When the batik is completely dry glue the piece to the front of the card. Write a Christmas message inside, and give the greeting as a special holiday gift.

Crafts

The diversity among India's millions of people is reflected in the great variety of artwork found in the country. Different religions, cultures, and language groups have contributed carved ivory figures, brass sculpture, silver jewelry, pottery, woven fabrics of silk and cotton, paintings, wood carvings, and lacquerware. Directions for two easy craft items incorporating Indian techniques and traditions are presented for use during the Christmas season.

Clay Dipa Lamps

Diwali is an Indian festival celebrated in late October or early November. Its origins are obscured in folklore and legend. Light is associated with the holiday, and an item most identified with this time of the year is the *Diwali*, or *dipa*, lamp. These small clay pots line windowsills, balconies, rooftops, and garden paths of homes and businesses. Since Christmas celebrates the coming of Jesus, the true light of all people, use clay prayer lamps during the Christmas season.

Materials:

- ✧ Self-hardening clay
- ✧ Wicks
- ✧ Lamp oil or vegetable oil
- ✧ Votive candles

Method:

To form a prayer lamp, take a small amount of clay, about the size of a walnut, and place it in the palm of your hand. Gently rotate the material around until a small round bowl is shaped. With the thumb and forefinger, press one area of the rim together to form a V or U shape. Allow the pot to air dry and harden. Place a small votive candle in the center of the clay pot, light it and use the piece as a prayer lamp. A wick and oil may be used instead of a candle. Coil the wick and put it in the bowl with one end extending one-half inch past the lip of the pot. Pour in just enough oil to cover the wick coil.

Mica Inset Embroidery Ornament

Embroidery, one of the traditional crafts of India, is often embellished with small, mirror-like pieces sewn into the design. Mica, translucent or transparent mineral crystals that flake into thin layers, is often used. This shiny substance creates a looking glass effect. Create a Christmas tree ornament to simulate this type of art. Instead of mica pieces use metal foil or metallic plastic sewing trims to add interest and beauty to the embroidery.

Materials:

- ✧ Cloth
- ✧ Scissors
- ✧ Embroidery thread
- ✧ Needle
- ✧ Metal foil or metallic plastic circles

- ✧ Drapery ring, wooden or metal
- ✧ Glue
- ✧ Ribbon, yarn, or string
- ✧ Pencil

Method:

Select a frame for the Christmas tree ornament. A round wooden or metal drapery ring works well. Cut a piece of fabric to fit the ring. The material may be a bright color, such as red, orange, or purple, colors often used in Indian embroidery, or it can be white or off-white to accent the colors of the decoration.

Plan the design for the ornament. Try making a symbol associated with the celebration of Christmas in India, like a dipa lamp, or a familiar holiday decoration, such as a star. Sketch the plan on the cloth with pencil. Decide on the placement of the metal or plastic pieces. Thread the needle and sew the outline of the symbol onto the cloth using a cross stitch or running stitch. The thread color can complement or contrast with the colors of the cloth and insets. Attach the shiny pieces by sewing through the small holes or over or through the metal or plastic pieces.

Spread glue around the edge of one side of the drapery ring. Place it on top of the right side of the embroidered piece of cloth. Thread yarn, string or ribbon through the top of the ornament and hang it on a Christmas tree or wreath.

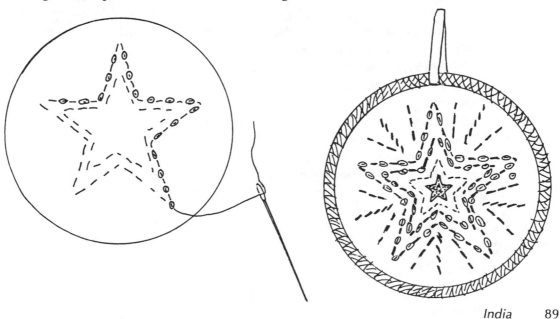

Carols

Indian Christians sing traditional carols from other countries as well as their own compositions. The music is accompanied by Indian instruments. Part of the purpose of carol programs in India is to proclaim the gospel story to those who haven't heard it. Two carols that would be appropriate for telling the story of Jesus' birth are "O Come, All Ye Faithful" and "What Child Is This?"

Story

Christians in India celebrate Christmas with symbols and gestures borrowed from their Hindu neighbors. Bells, clappers, drums, and dancing are part of the celebration. Incense is burned as offering and purification during the ritual. The prayer service below offers an opportunity to tell the story of the nativity using some of these Indian traditions.

Materials:

✧ Incense	✧ Bible
✧ Incense container	✧ Music for selected songs
✧ Matches	✧ Accompaniment
✧ Table	✧ Bells
✧ Table covering (use batik cloth if possible)	✧ Clappers
	✧ Drums

Method:

Gathering Prayer

Leader: God, our Creator and life sustainer, you love us in all things. Give each of us gathered here a deep awareness of your love for all people everywhere. Lead us with great sensitivity to the poor of this world and to those who do not believe because they have not heard the story.

The Christmas story of Emmanuel's entrance into this world is a universal story. It is heard in many languages, celebrated with many customs, and remembered through different rituals. Call us now to enter fully into this celebration. Like our brothers and sisters in India we bring bells and clappers, drums and dancing, that we may hear the story with new ears.

By the power of the Spirit, may we grow in love and in truth and be called to a life of passion, worthy of the story and the message it gives to the whole world.

All: Amen.

Reading

Mt 1:18–24; Mt 2:1–12

Before the reading begins, place a bowl of burning incense on the prayer table or somewhere in the prayer space.

Song

"O Come, All Ye Faithful"

Invite people to stand, hold hands, and form a circle, or several small circles. Direct the group to move slowly to the music in a clockwise direction as the carol is played or sung. Use bells, clappers, and drums to accompany the music. The song can also be danced.

Ritual Action

Invite those gathered to form small groups of four or five. Families can remain as one group. Encourage the people to share what the Christmas story means to them. How do they celebrate the day? What do they do to make it holy? Allow enough time for each person to say something.

Litany of Praise

Invite the people to respond "We praise you, O God" to the following invocations.

Gentle One
O Living Word
God of Christmas
God of all people
Giver of gifts
Mystery of life
God of hope
Emmanuel, the promise
Healing bread
Seeker of stillness
God of Wonder
Breath of new life
Womb of all
God of the story
God of laughter
Child within
Creator of all seasons
Heart of mercy

Closing Prayer

Leader: O God of the story, you are praised in many tongues and with many names. We thank you for sharing the Word and for giving it life. Through that Word we have been given life. Continue to enrich the stories of our own hearts, that the examples of our lives will be a witness to many people.

Closing Ritual

Invite those gathered to share a sign of peace with each other.

Closing Song: "What Child Is This?"

Culinary

■

Indian food is known for its spiciness. In some dishes, a single spice is used, while in others more than a dozen varieties are part of the cooking process. Try a recipe for a traditional meal, meat and potato curry, to get a taste of Indian culture.

Another common ingredient found in Indian recipes is yogurt. Yogurt, with its high protein, is an essential staple in the diet of many Indians, particularly if they're vegetarians. A recipe for sweet banana and yogurt salad, a treat reserved for special occasions, is provided.

Serve both of these dishes with spicy, flavorful tea during the Christmas season.

Meat and Potato Curry

Since the flavors of curry improve with sitting, this dish may be made in advance, refrigerated, and reheated.

Ingredients:

⟡ 1/4 cup margarine

⟡ 2 pounds beef roast, cubed

⟡ 1 large onion, chopped

⟡ 1/2 teaspoon caraway seed

⟡ 1/2 teaspoon peppercorns

⟡ 1 large bay leaf, crushed

⟡ 1/2 teaspoon ground ginger

⟡ 1/2 teaspoon ground turmeric

⟡ 1/2 teaspoon ground coriander

⟡ 1 clove garlic, chopped

⟡ 1/4 teaspoon ground cloves
   or 2–3 whole cloves

⟡ 1 cinnamon stick

⟡ Salt to taste

⟡ 2 cardamom pods, optional

⟡ 3–4 cups tomatoes, chopped,
   or tomato juice

⟡ 2–3 potatoes, cubed

⟡ 1–2 tablespoons curry powder

Method:

Melt the margarine in a saucepan. Add the beef cubes and brown well. Add and brown the chopped onion, caraway seed, peppercorns, bay leaf, ginger, turmeric, coriander, garlic, cloves, cinnamon, salt, and cardamom. Stir in the tomatoes or tomato juice and simmer the mixture for one hour. Add the potatoes, curry powder, and additional salt, if desired, and cook until the meat and potatoes are tender. Water may be added if needed.

Instead of beef, 2 1/2 pounds of chicken pieces may be used in this recipe. Reduce the first cooking time from one hour to 30–35 minutes.

Remove the whole spices before serving or while eating. Serves six.*

---

* Schlabach, Joetta Handrich. *Extending the Table. . . A World Community Cookbook*. Scottdale, PA: Herald Press, 1991, p. 246. Used by permission.

Sweet Banana and Yogurt Salad

Ingredients:

- ✧ 2 tablespoons slivered, blanched almonds
- ✧ 2 tablespoons seedless raisins
- ✧ 1/2 cup water
- ✧ 1 1/2 cups plain yogurt
- ✧ 1/2 cup sour cream

- ✧ 3–4 tablespoons honey
- ✧ 1/8 teaspoon ground cardamom or grated nutmeg
- ✧ 1 medium banana, peeled and thinly sliced

Method:

Place the almonds and raisins in a small bowl and add 1/2 cup boiling water. Soak for fifteen minutes and drain.

Mix almonds and raisins with the yogurt, sour cream, honey, and cardamom or nutmeg. Gently fold the banana slices into the yogurt mixture. Chill thoroughly before serving.

Game

Play a matching game to review Indian Christmas customs and traditions. Draw a line from the statement on the left to the word on the right that best answers or describes the phrase.

1. One of the many religions found in India
2. Method used to present the gospel story on Christmas Eve
3. Brightly colored plant used as a holiday decoration
4. White banner with a red cross in the center
5. Lines the roofs of Christian homes on Christmas Eve
6. Opportunity to invite non-Christian friends and family to church
7. Follows the Christmas Eve worship service
8. Traditional gift at Christmas
9. Method of applying wax and dyes to create works of art
10. Spice used in many Indian foods

A. Poinsettia
B. Candles
C. Clothing
D. Curry
E. Worship service
F. Hindu
G. Party
H. Christmas flag
I. Batik
J. Drama

•JAPAN•

Country Information

■

*J*apan lies in the Pacific Ocean, off the east coast of Asia. The country is made up of a chain of rugged, mountainous islands — four main islands and more than 3,900 smaller ones.

Japan is one of the most densely populated nations in the world with 123.5 million inhabitants. The Japanese people practice Eastern religions such as Buddhism, Shintoism, and Confucianism. Only 1.5 million people in the country are Christians. Approximately sixty percent of these are Protestant, while forty percent are Roman Catholic.

Few natural resources are found in Japan and only a small percentage of the land is suitable for cultivation. Farmers grow rice, the national food, and tea, as well as mulberry leaves to feed to silkworms. Major industries include machinery and equipment, metals and metal products, textiles, autos, chemicals, and electrical equipment.*

---

* Adams, Juanita, Editor. *Background Notes: Japan*. Washington, DC: United States Department of State, 1989.

Flag

Japan's flag is a red circle, representing the sun, on a white field.

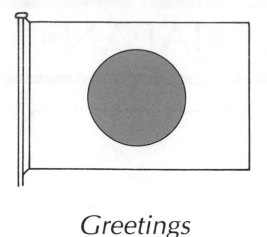

Greetings

The Christmas greeting in Japanese is *Meri Kurisumasu*. The greeting of peace is *heiwa*.

Customs

Christmas was first celebrated in Japan in the middle of the sixteenth century by the converts of Spanish and Portuguese missionaries. Since the early 1900s, the holiday has been observed on a larger scale, but the religious activities associated with the season are mainly confined to churches and schools sponsored by foreign missionaries.

For most Japanese people, Christmas is a secular festival. Store windows are decorated with Christmas trees and trimmed with red and green paper holly and bells. Since many Christmas toys and ornaments are made in this island nation, buying and selling holiday gifts and accessories is an important part of Japanese business.

For the small Christian population of Japan, Christmas provides a time to share the true meaning of the season with non-Christian friends. The gospel message is proclaimed through elaborate Sunday School pageants and programs and worship services. A festive tea party follows. Gifts and cards designed to help the receiver know more about the Savior are often given. Christmas in Japan is a time when Jesus comes with new power into the hearts of the believers. It is also a joyful season during which Christ comes into the lives of people who are experiencing this love for the first time.

New Year observances, from January 1 through January 3, are the most important and most elaborate of Japan's annual events. Although customs differ in various locations throughout the islands, homes are usually decorated and the holiday is celebrated by family gatherings, visits to shrines or temples, and formal calls on relatives and friends.

New Year decorations, traditionally a sacred rope of straw with dangling white paper strips, are hung over the front door to prevent evil spirits from entering the home. Pine branches, bamboo stalks, and plum branches are generally placed at the gateway to ensure prosperity and good health for the coming year. A special altar is set up in the home and piled high with Japanese foods in honor of the *toshigami*, the deity of the coming year.

Year-end fairs are held toward the end of December for purchasing holiday items. New Year cards are sent to family, friends, and acquaintances. On New Year's Eve, families gather for holiday meals. Many people visit Buddhist temples to hear the temple bells rung 108 times at midnight to dispel the evil of the past year.

January 1 involves rituals and religious observances connected with doing things for the first time in the new year, such as serving the first meal and offering the first prayer.

Crèche

In Christian communities in Japan, the Christmas story is told through elaborate programs and pageants. Children of all ages are involved in playing parts and singing songs that proclaim the good news of the birth of the Savior for all people.

Experience the story of the nativity through the use of drama. Create an easy script using the story in Luke 2:1–20. The goal is to break the Bible verses into character parts so that the passage will be more understandable to those hearing it. Try to adhere as closely as possible to the words of the Bible.

Step One: Identify the characters in the passage.

Step Two: Find all the quotes in the passage. Match a character to each of them. Try to break long passages into several parts.

Step Three: Write lines for any portion of the passage that could be assigned to a specific person. Look for verbs that suggest that the narrative could be written in dialogue form.

Step Four: Add one or more narrators to provide information between the speaking parts.

A sample script based on Luke 2:1–20 is provided. The words are adapted from the New International Version of the Bible.

Take turns playing the parts: Narrator, Caesar Augustus, Joseph, Mary, angels, and shepherds. Drape strips of fabric over the actors' and actresses' heads and shoulders to create simple costumes.

Sample Script

Caesar Augustus: A census must be taken of the entire Roman world. Everyone must go to his or her own town to register.

Joseph:	Mary, we must go from Nazareth to Bethlehem, because I am of the house and line of David.
Mary:	It will be a long journey for me since my baby is due to be born very soon.
Narrator:	Upon arriving in Bethlehem, Joseph and Mary discovered that there was no room for them in the inn.
Joseph:	We will stay in the stable where the cattle are kept.
Narrator:	While they were there, the time came for the baby to be born, and Mary gave birth to her firstborn, a son.
Mary:	Let us wrap the baby in cloths to keep him warm.
Joseph:	We can place him in the manger.
Narrator:	There were shepherds living out in the fields nearby, keeping watch over their flocks.
Shepherd One:	One night, an angel of the Lord appeared to us, and the glory of the Lord shone around us, and we were terrified.
Angel:	Do not be afraid, I bring you good news of great joy that will be for all the people. Today in the town of David a Savior has been born to you; he is Christ the Lord. This will be a sign to you: You will find a baby wrapped in cloths and lying in a manger.
Shepherd Two:	A great company of the heavenly host appeared with the angel, praising God and saying:
Angels:	Glory to God in the highest, and on earth peace to men on whom his favor rests.
Narrator:	When the angels returned to heaven, the shepherds said to one another:
Shepherd One:	Let's go to Bethlehem and see this thing that has happened, which the Lord has told us about.
Shepherd Two:	We hurried off and found Mary and Joseph, and the baby, who was lying in the manger.
Shepherd One:	After we worshipped the baby, we spread the word concerning what had been told to us about this child.
Shepherd Two:	All who heard it were amazed at what we said to them.
Mary:	I will treasure all of these things and ponder them in my heart.
Narrator:	The shepherds returned, glorifying and praising God for all that they had heard and seen, which was just as they had been told.

Gift Giver

■

Hoteiosho, a Japanese god with eyes in the back of his head, brings gifts to good children. He is pictured much like Santa Claus.

In Christian communities, people spend several weeks before the holiday preparing presents to be delivered to hospital patients during the Christmas season.

Missionaries hold Christmas parties for the children in their apartment buildings and neighborhoods and distribute gifts with religious significance.

Card

━━━━━━ ■ ━━━━━━

Although the custom of sending Christmas cards is gaining popularity among the people of Japan, they generally observe the tradition of mailing New Year's greetings to virtually all of their relatives, friends, and acquaintances.

Typically, the Japanese New Year's card is made from a regular government issued postcard. Many families design their own postcards and have them printed. Some government issue cards are stamped with lottery numbers that may enable the recipient to win prizes. These and other unique designs are sold for one *yen* above the regular price, with the extra money going to charity.

New Year's greetings allow the sender to extend wishes for a happy holiday, to thank the receiver for past favors, and to solicit good will for the coming year.

Design a postcard to send during the Christmas season. Write a verse using a traditional style of Japanese poetry, such as *Haiku* or *Waka*. *Haiku*, a three line, seventeen syllable poem, emphasizes nature. It expresses the essence of a sight or an idea in the most succinct manner possible. *Waka* is a poem containing thirty one syllables, in six lines, which explores a variety of human emotions.

Materials:

    ✧ Postcards   ✧ Pens

    ✧ Paper   ✧ Markers

Method:

The pattern for *Haiku* is:

Line One - 5 syllables

Line Two - 7 syllables

Line Three - 5 syllables

An example of a Christmas *Haiku* is:

In the cold winter

Hearts are warmed at Christmas time

By God's gift of love.

Waka's formula is:

Line One - 4 syllables

Line Two - 6 syllables

Line Three - 7 syllables

Line Four - 7 syllables

Line Five - 5 syllables

Line Six - 3 syllables

A sample Christmas *Waka* is:

I am joyful.

Christmas is here again.

Celebrate the birth of Christ.

Share the news of Jesus birth.

Gladness fills my heart.

There is peace.

Compose a Christmas *Haiku* or *Waka* and write it on the front of a plain postcard. Using markers or other art materials, illustrate the message of the poem, if desired. Add a personal greeting to the other side of the card and mail or deliver it as a special holiday wish.

Crafts

Directions for two craft projects incorporating Japanese art techniques are provided. Both use paper as the primary media. Cherry blossoms, found in the landscape and gardens of Japan, are also the subject of much of the art of the country. Create a picture of these beautiful flowers using the technique of *sumi-e* painting. In this type of art, the importance of white space around the subject is stressed. Brush strokes are kept to a minimum and the power of the picture is in its simplicity.

Cherry Blossom Paintings

Materials:

  ✧ Construction paper   ✧ Container for paint
  ✧ Sticks, six inches long   ✧ Glue
  ✧ Tempera paint, brown   ✧ Tissue paper or facial tissue, pink

Method:

Choose a piece of construction paper to use as the background for the drawing. It could be blue to represent the sky, or white or off-white to emphasize the colors in the picture. Use a stick, about six inches long, for a paint brush. Pour brown tempera paint into a shallow container. Dip one end of the stick into the paint and use it to draw bare branches on the piece of paper. Remember to keep the picture simple and to allow for white space around the subject.

While the paint is drying, make cherry blossoms to add to the branches. Tear pink tissue paper or facial tissue into small pieces. Squeeze dots of glue onto the branches and press bits of tissue over it to produce fluffy blossoms.

Hang the picture on a wall or bulletin board. The technique can also be used on the front of a card or as the design for a unique piece of wrapping paper.

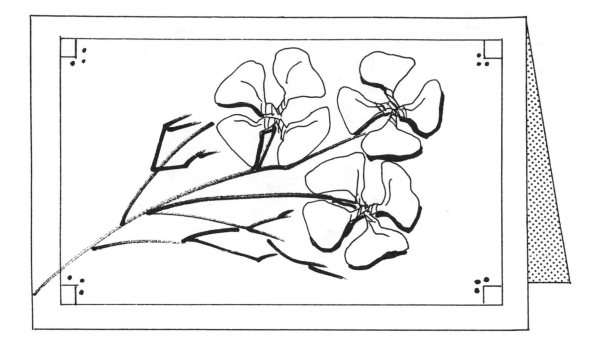

Origami Stars

Materials:

- ✧ Paper
- ✧ Scissors
- ✧ Paper punch
- ✧ Thread, string, or yarn

Method:

Origami is the Japanese art of paper folding. Try making a Christmas star to use as an ornament. *Origami* paper is available at craft stores. Any lightweight paper will also work for the project.

Begin with a perfectly square piece of paper. Fold it in half to form a triangle. With the point facing up and the crease at the bottom, label the left corner A, the right corner B, and the top point C. Use the illustrations as a guide for the remainder of the procedure.

Fold point B to point C. Unfold. Fold A over so that its point touches the edge of the crease made by the previous fold, labeled D in the diagram. The two new corners are labeled E and F. Pick up point B and fold it along the edge E-D. Fold C-F along the edge E-B. Using scissors, cut off point E diagonally according to the dotted line in the diagram. This small piece of paper becomes the *origami* star. Unfold the star. Crease the five long lines to accentuate the shape.

To use the star as an ornament, make a hole near the end of one point. Loop string, thread, or yarn through it.

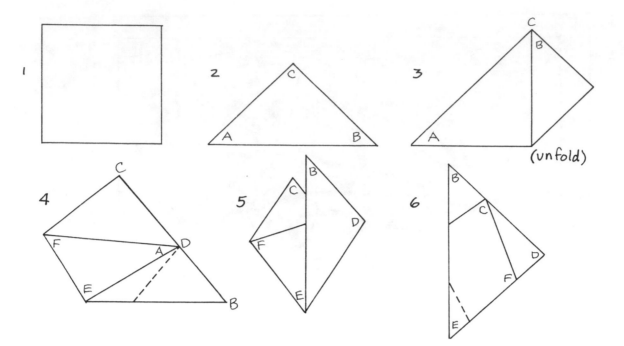

Carols

Most of the Christmas songs sung in Japan are variations of Western hymns. The 1990 edition of *The Presbyterian Hymnal* (Louisville: Westminster/John Knox Press, 1990) contains two Japanese carols. The three verses of "Sleep Fast Asleep" are printed with Japanese and English words. The other hymn is "Joyful Christmas Day Is Here."

Story

The Story of the Grateful Crane, by Jennifer Bartoli (Chicago: Albert Whitman, 1977), tells the story of a Japanese farmer and his wife.

As he is walking home one day, he notices a crane trapped in the snow and stops to free the bird. Later that evening there is a knock on the door of his house. A beautiful young girl asks for a place to spend the night.

When the man and his wife provide hospitality to her, the young woman asks if they will take her for their daughter. In gratitude, the girl weaves beautiful cloth for the poor couple to sell, and they are paid large sums of money for the material.

In time the couple discovers that the young woman is the crane who is repaying the man for saving her life.

Culinary

■

Christmas dinner in many Japanese homes consists of turkey and all the trimmings. In other families, a more traditional meal of rice, raw or smoked fish, bean cakes, pickled vegetables, and seaweed might be served and eaten with chopsticks.

Recipes for two favorite Japanese dishes are included. Try chicken fried rice and almond cookies during the twelve days of Christmas. Serve them with tea.

Chicken Fried Rice

Rice, the basic food of Japan, is usually part of every meal. Chicken fried rice is a favorite way to serve it.

Ingredients:

- 1/4 cup vegetable oil
- 4 1/2 cups cold, cooked short-grain rice
- 1 1/2 cups cold, shredded cooked chicken
- 1/3 cup diced yellow onion
- 1/3 cup diced celery
- 1/4 teaspoon salt
- 2 eggs, well beaten
- 1 teaspoon soy sauce

Method:

Heat oil in skillet or wok. Stir fry the rice until thoroughly heated, and then add the chicken, onion, celery, and salt. Stir fry for five minutes. Mix the beaten eggs with the soy sauce and stir fry until cooked and well blended. Serve immediately. Makes four servings.

Almond Cookies

A favorite Japanese dessert is the almond cookie. Try this tasty treat as an ending to a Japanese meal, or as a delicious snack.

Ingredients:

- 3 cups sifted flour
- 1 cup sugar
- 1 cup shortening
- 4 tablespoons corn syrup, molasses, or honey
- 1 egg
- 3 tablespoons almond extract
- 1 1/2 teaspoons baking soda
- 1 cup blanched almonds

Method:

Cream the shortening and sugar together. Add the beaten egg. Slowly add flour, baking soda, almond extract, and syrup to the mixture and blend until smooth.

Take a small piece of the dough and roll it into a ball. Continue until all the dough has been used. Flatten each ball into a thick cookie. Place an almond in the center of each piece.

Bake on a greased cookie sheet in a 375 degree oven for about twenty minutes. Makes about four dozen cookies.

Game

Although kite making originated in China, it has become a very popular folk-art and sport in the country of Japan. Many Japanese kites are shaped and decorated to resemble animals and insects, while others portray abstract or humorous motifs. Kites come in all shapes and sizes. Sometimes they are so large that they require teams of people to handle them.

On Children's Day, formerly called Boys' Day, which is observed May 5, each Japanese family that has a child flies a kite in the shape of a fish from a pole attached to its house. Many kite flying games and competitions are held on this national holiday as well as throughout the year.

Make a kite to give as a Christmas gift or to enjoy as a decoration. A fish would be a good design for the kite. Fish are often depicted in Japanese art since Japan is surrounded by water. The ocean provides a livelihood and food for millions of people.

Materials:

       ◇ Paper bags   ◇ Tissue paper

       ◇ Scissors   ◇ Crepe paper

       ◇ Markers   ◇ Paper punch

       ◇ Glue   ◇ String

       ◇ Construction paper

Method:

One paper bag is needed for each kite. It can be any size and color, however a lunch bag is a good size to use for the project. Colors will show up better on white bags than on brown ones.

Form the fish's mouth by cutting a large circle out of the bottom of the bag. Cut two large round shapes out of black construction paper and glue one to each side of the bag to serve as eyes. Decorate the fish with markers and tissue paper pieces.

Cut scallops along the open edge of the bag to form a tail. Glue long strips of colored crepe paper to this end of the bag to add interest and variety to the tail.

When the decorations are completed, punch two holes in the bottom of each sack in the corners above the mouth. Tie a piece of string through the holes to make a handle.

Take the kite outside and fly it in the wind, hang the fish on the wall or ceiling, or give it as a special Christmas gift. Miniature kites, made from very small bags, can be used as ornaments on a Christmas tree.

▪MEXICO▪

Country Information

▪

*T*he United Mexican States share their northern border with the United States of America and cover an area three times the size of the state of Texas. Mexico City is the capital. The topography of Mexico ranges from low desert plains and jungle-like coastal strips to high plateaus and rugged mountains. Its climate varies from tropical to desert.

Eighty-eight million people inhabit Mexico. Ethnic groups include Indian-Spanish (Mestizo), Native American, and Caucasian. Ninety-seven percent of the population practices the Roman Catholic religion. The other three percent are Protestant.

Mexico is rich in mineral and energy resources. These include petroleum, silver, copper, gold, lead, zinc, natural gas, and timber. Many agricultural products come from Mexico, such as corn, beans, oil seeds, feedgrains, fruit, cotton, coffee, sugarcane, and winter vegetables. Industries include manufacturing, services, commerce, transportation, communications, petroleum, and mining.*

---

* Adams, Juanita, Editor. *Background Notes: Mexico*. Washington, DC: United States Department of State, 1990.

Flag

Green, white, and red vertical bands form the field of Mexico's flag. An eagle in the center holds a snake in its beak and is perched on a cactus.

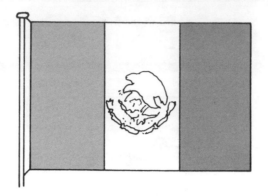

Greetings

The official language of Mexico is Spanish. The Christmas greeting is *Feliz Navidad*. The greeting of peace is *paz*.

Customs

Poinsettias, *piñatas*, *pastorelas*, and *posadas* are all part of the exciting way in which the season of Christmas is celebrated in Mexico. In regal mansions and cardboard shacks, humble chapels and stately cathedrals, the blend of Spanish and Indian culture enlivens old customs with new variations.

The Christmas season begins on December 16 when the nine day *posada* processions start. The word *posada* means resting place, lodging, or inn. The processions re-enact Mary and Joseph's journey from Nazareth to Bethlehem and their attempt to find a place to stay.

Posadas had their beginnings in the sixteenth century when St. Ignatius Loyola said Christmas prayers, called novenas, for nine consecutive days. The number nine represents Mary's nine months of pregnancy. In 1580, Saint John of the Cross made a religious pageant out of the novena. Spanish missionaries eventually brought the tradition of the *posada* to Mexico.

Posadas are festive community events. Friends, relatives, and neighbors all participate. As soon as it is dark, families travel to one another's homes. A child dressed as an angel heads the procession. More costumed children follow and the first few in the crowd carry figures of Mary and Joseph on a small litter decorated with twigs of pine. Adults and musicians take up the rear of the parade. All participants carry lighted candles.

When the people reach a home, they divide into two groups: the pilgrims and the innkeepers. The pilgrims sing traditional songs asking for shelter. If the innkeepers turn them away, the group repeats the ritual at one or more homes until the whole group is finally invited inside. The dialogue may take place in this manner.

"Who knocks at my door, so late in the night?"

"We are pilgrims, without shelter, and we want only a place to rest."

"Go somewhere else and disturb me not again."

"But the night is very cold. We have come from afar, and we are very tired."

"But who are you? I know you not."

"I am Joseph of Nazareth, a carpenter, and with me is Mary, my wife, who will be the mother of the Son of God."

"Then come into my humble home, and welcome! And may the Lord give shelter to my soul when I leave this world."

After the travelers are welcomed, a prayer similar to the following is offered:

"O God, who, in coming to save us, didst not disdain a humble stable, grant that we may never close our hearts when thou art knocking so that we may be made worthy to be received into thy sight when our hour comes."*

A party follows with food, fireworks, and the breaking of a *piñata*.

Individual families carry on *posada* processions by knocking on the door of each room and finally being admitted to the room where the nativity scene is set up. On Christmas Eve, the image of the Christ Child is carried and laid in the manger.

In many parts of the country *pastorelas* are performed. These are a Mexican version of Europe's medieval miracle plays. They may last from one-half hour to many days. The plot involves the shepherds' pilgrimage to Bethlehem to see the Christ Child. The plays present a mixture of religious teachings and Indian and Mexican folklore.

Christmas Eve is observed with a solemn midnight church service. Christmas Day is welcomed with bells, whistles, and firecrackers.

Two other important days during the Christmas season are December 28, the Day of the Innocents, which is observed with pranks, much like April Fool's Day is celebrated, and Epiphany, January 6, when gifts are exchanged.

Crèche

Nativity scenes, called *nacimientos*, are set up on December 16, the day the *posadas* begin. They may be found in homes, churches, store windows, government offices, plazas, and public parks.

In homes, an altar covered with pine branches and moss is erected in an area of one room and the nativity scene is created on it. Generally, there is total incongruity in the scene. There may be tropical blossoms in a snow scene, centuries-old Spanish explorers, a modern day taco seller, and characters from many Bible stories. Often parents choose a shepherd figure to represent each child in the household. At the end of each day, the figures are moved a step closer to the manger if the children were good.

---

* Wernecke, Herbert H. *Christmas Customs Around the World.* Philadelphia: Westminster Press, 1979, p. 83.

The baby Jesus is put into the manger on Christmas Eve. Before the manger scene is packed away for the year, a ceremony takes place in which one girl in the family removes the baby Jesus, members of the household process to the church where the figure is blessed, and the group returns home.

Most Mexican nativity sets are made from clay. Try making one by following this easy method.

Materials:

- ✧ Clay
- ✧ Newspaper
- ✧ Wax paper
- ✧ Water
- ✧ Paper towels
- ✧ Plastic drop cloths
- ✧ Tempera paint, optional
- ✧ Shellac, optional
- ✧ Brushes, optional
- ✧ Evergreen branches
- ✧ Moss

Advance Preparation:

- ✧ Cover the floor of the work area with the drop cloths.
- ✧ Place newspaper on the tables of the work area. Set sheets of waxed paper on top of the newspaper.

Method:

Decide which figures will be made. All of the characters could be from the nativity story, or in keeping with Mexican tradition, they might represent current or historic people.

Take a small amount of clay and form it into the shape of a ball. Work with the clay to sense how it feels and responds. Mold the clay into the desired shapes. Push and pull the clay into figures two to three inches high. Roll clay into a coil to use as arms and add them to the body by using a small amount of water like glue. Make hair, facial features, and decorations with clay, too. Allow the clay to harden. The hardened figures may be painted in bright colors and designs and covered with shellac.

Create a nativity scene with the figures. Spread evergreen branches and moss on a table and place the characters in it.

Gift Giver

In Mexican homes small gifts for the children are left by the manger scene on Christmas morning. The real gifts are given by the Three Kings on Epiphany, January 6. On the night of January 5, children fill their shoes with straw from the manger and leave it as an offering for the camels. In the morning, the straw is gone and the shoes are buried in mounds of gifts.

Card

On Christmas Day, service people such as garbage collectors deliver handmade greeting cards to their patrons. The recipient offers money or small gifts and candy for the person's children. Often the cards are decorated with the beautiful Mexican plant, the poinsettia.

Several legends are associated with the poinsettia plant. One involves a young boy who wanted to visit the manger at his village church. Since he was poor and had no gift to bring to the Christ Child, he picked some green branches along the way and decided to offer them to the baby Jesus. As soon as the branches were cut, they sprouted bright red leaves. When the boy placed the gift at the crib, the Virgin Mary gestured her loving approval and golden stars began to twinkle on her robe and in the center of the leaves. The poinsettia has since been known as the flower of Christmas.

Sponge paint handmade cards that incorporate the bright and beautiful design of the poinsettia.

Materials:

- ✧ Tempera paint; red, green, yellow
- ✧ Water
- ✧ Liquid detergent
- ✧ Plastic containers
- ✧ Paper
- ✧ Sponges
- ✧ Scissors
- ✧ Clothespins, spring-type
- ✧ Markers

Advance Preparation:

- ✧ Pre-mix tempera paint to a medium consistency. Add a squirt of laundry detergent to aid clean-up. Place each color in a separate container.
- ✧ Cut the sponges into 1" x 2" pieces.
- ✧ Clip a clothespin to one end of each sponge.

Method:

Choose a piece of paper to use for the card and fold it in half. To sponge paint a poinsettia on the front of it, hold the end of the clothespin and dip the sponge into the red paint. Use a small amount of paint for each stroke. Lightly press the paint onto the paper to form the red leaves. Add green leaves and yellow stamens. The shapes may be outlined with marker.

Write a verse about the legend of the poinsettia inside the card. Offer the special greeting to a family member or a friend.

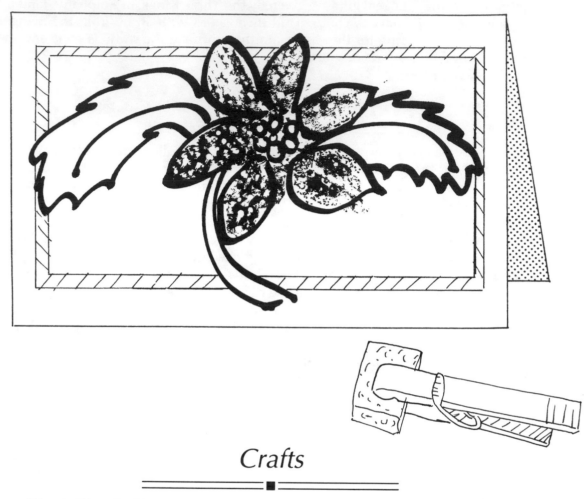

Crafts

Ojos de Dios, God's eyes, have been made by the Huichol Indians of Mexico for hundreds of years. Brightly colored yarn is woven around a simple frame of crossed sticks. The central diamond pattern symbolizes the eye of God and the bands of color around it stand for the wisdom and light coming from the eye.

Colorful yarn wrapped birds and other small animals are made in many villages in Mexico. They are used as ornaments and decorations. Although the bodies are often made of pottery, they can also be formed from papier-mâché.

Directions for both these crafts are provided below.

Ojo de Dios (God's Eye)

Materials:

◇ Sticks or dowel rods   ◇ Scissors
◇ Yarn

Method:

Form a cross with two sticks. Begin working with the color of yarn that will be the center of the eye. With one end of the yarn, tie the cross in place, using square knots. Wind the yarn forward and completely around one dowel. Bring the yarn back over the top of the stick. Move to the next dowel and make a circle of yarn around it. Continue going around each dowel in order. Pull the yarn tightly as the sticks are wrapped. Lay each yarn down next to the yarn before it. The yarn should lie in neat rows. To start a new color, cut the old color off and tie the new color onto the end of the previous yarn with a double knot. Stop winding before reaching the ends of the sticks. Tassels may be added to the ends.

Tiny God's eyes can be made from toothpicks and embroidery threads. The *Ojos de Dios* can be used as ornaments, or several can be combined to form a mobile.

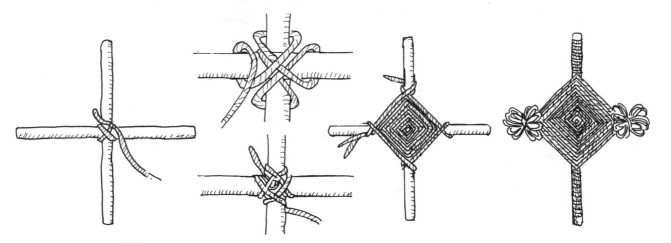

Yarn Wrapped Birds

Materials:

- ✧ Wallpaper paste
- ✧ Water
- ✧ Containers
- ✧ Stir stick
- ✧ Newspaper
- ✧ White glue
- ✧ Brush, small
- ✧ Yarn, heavyweight
- ✧ Scissors
- ✧ Pins

Method:

Begin the body of the bird by using a papier-mâché process. Combine the wallpaper paste and water according to the package directions. Stir the mixture until it is smooth and well blended. In another container, mix one part of the paste with one part white glue.

Crumple sheets of newspaper and form them into the shape of a small bird. Tear or cut additional newspaper into long, narrow strips. Dip individual strips of newspaper into the wallpaper paste and glue mixture and cover the entire body of the bird with them. Continue this procedure until several layers have been formed. Let the bird dry completely.

Tie a piece of heavy yarn around the body and form a loop at the top to be used to hang the ornament. Add brightly colored yarn to the body. Brush glue onto a small area of the animal. Make designs — circles, ovals, leaves, and flowers — with the yarn and attach them to the bird. It may be helpful to pin the yarn in place while it is drying. Cover the entire body with yarn.

Make a variety of different birds and animals by using this process.

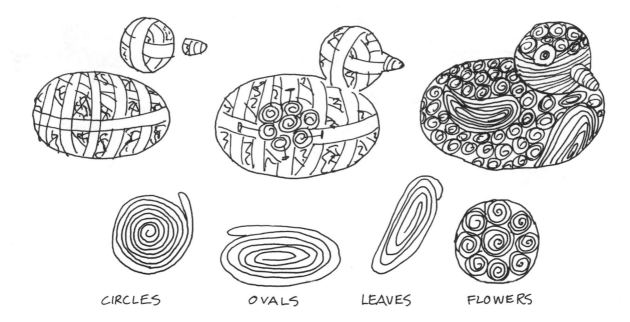

CIRCLES   OVALS   LEAVES   FLOWERS

Carols

Music in Mexico is often associated with the *posada* processions. "Pray Give Us Lodging" (*En Nombre del Cielo*) describes the events portrayed in the *posada*. "The Babe" (*El Rorro*) is a Mexican lullaby to the newborn Savior. Both these carols can be found in *The International Book of Christmas Carols* (Walter Ehret and George K. Evans, Brattleboro, VT: Stephen Greene Press, 1980).

Story

━━━━■━━━━

The Christmas Piñata by Jack Kent (New York: Parents' Magazine Press, 1975) tells the story of a potter who discovers that one of his newly formed clay containers has cracked while baking. He sets it in the corner and considers it useless. Maria, the potter's daughter, discovers the pot and chooses it to become the base of the Christmas *piñata*. Once it is filled, decorated, and hung, it becomes the center of attention and provides a source of joy and excitement for the children of the village.

Culinary

━━━━■━━━━

Christmas Eve dinner in Mexican homes takes place after a solemn midnight worship service at church. The meal generally consists of turkey, tortillas, vegetables, fried peppers, fruits, candies, and hot chocolate with vanilla and cinnamon. A special Christmas salad of fruits, nuts, beets, and sugar cane sprinkled with tiny colored candies might also be served.

On Epiphany, January 6, a crown shaped cake is part of a festive celebration. Traditionally, a small doll representing the Christ Child is baked into the cake and the person who finds it may keep it and is expected to give a party on February 2, another special holiday.

Serve a Mexican dinner during the twelve days of Christmas. Try these two recipes as part of the menu.

Holiday Flan

Flan is a rich custard dessert with a honey or carmel glaze.

Ingredients:

- ✧ 4 eggs
- ✧ 2 1/2 cups milk
- ✧ 1/2 cup honey
- ✧ 1 teaspoon vanilla
- ✧ 1 to 2 tablespoons warmed honey or maple syrup

Method:

In a medium bowl, beat the eggs until foamy. In a small saucepan, heat the milk and honey together just to simmering, then add the vanilla.

In a slow, thin stream, beat the milk mixture into the eggs. Pour the mixture into a buttered 9" layer cake pan or flan pan. Place in a large, shallow pan or baking dish filled with hot water to a depth of one-half inch. Bake at 325 degrees for thirty-five to forty minutes, or until the center is fairly firm. Glaze with the honey.

Makes six servings.

Holiday Fruit Compote

This fruit dish can be served hot or cold with a meal or as a dessert.

Ingredients:

- ✦ 1/2 pineapple, peeled and chopped
- ✦ 4 pears, seeded and chopped
- ✦ 2 apples, seeded and chopped
- ✦ 1 navel orange
- ✦ 1 cup cranberries
- ✦ 2 cups apple cider
- ✦ 1/2 teaspoon cinnamon
- ✦ 1/4 teaspoon grated nutmeg

Method:

Place the pineapple, pears, and apples in a large ovenproof casserole with cover.
Cut the orange in half. Peel one half and chop the flesh, removing any seeds. Place the chopped orange in the casserole with the pineapple, pears, and apples.

Coarsely chop the remaining orange half, including the peel, removing any seeds. Place this, along with the cranberries, cider, and spices, in a blender. Process on medium speed until the mixture is smooth.

Mix the blended mixture with the fruits in the casserole. Cover and bake in a 400 degree oven for forty minutes. Serve hot.

Makes eight servings.

Game

Following the festive *posada* processions, Mexican children gather to break a *piñata*. A *piñata* is a papier-mâché figure stuffed with candy, peanuts, fruit, and small toys.

The custom of the *piñata* began in Italy, spread to Spain, and was brought to Mexico by Spanish explorers. Priests often ended the Christmas Eve mass with the grand finale of having those gathered smash a *piñata*.

In Mexican cities, towns, and villages *piñatas* are a special part of the celebration of Christmas. The *piñata* is strung up by a rope running through a hook or pulley. One end of the rope is left free so it can be moved up and down. Children crowd around, sing songs, and demand goodies. One child at a time is blindfolded, given a large stick, and twirled around until dizzy. Each person tries to hit and break the *piñata*, but the adult keeps raising and lowering it. Each person is given three tries. Finally, the *piñata* breaks and everything falls out. The children scramble to retrieve the treasures and trinkets.*

Directions are provided here for constructing a *piñata* from the base of a brown paper grocery bag.

Christmas in Mexico. Chicago: World Book, 1976, p. 33.

Materials:

- ◇ Brown paper grocery bag, large
- ◇ Small toys
- ◇ Wrapped candies
- ◇ Peanuts
- ◇ Rope or cord
- ◇ Thread
- ◇ Newspaper
- ◇ White glue
- ◇ Bucket, small
- ◇ Water
- ◇ Waxed paper
- ◇ Brushes
- ◇ Poster paints
- ◇ Construction paper
- ◇ Tissue paper or crepe paper
- ◇ Tape
- ◇ Scissors
- ◇ Broom
- ◇ Blindfold
- ◇ Stick, large

Method:

Fill a large brown paper bag with small toys, wrapped candies, and peanuts. Gather the open end of the bag and tie a long piece of heavy cord or rope tightly around this end.

Using sewing thread, wrap it around the bag in every direction to provide added strength.

Tear newspaper into strips. Pour glue into a small bucket. Dilute the glue with water. Tear a long piece of waxed paper and lay newspaper strips on it. Brush one side of the strips with the diluted glue mixture. Place the glued side of the strips onto the bag covering the thread completely, up to the tie. Allow the bag to dry overnight.

Paint the bag in one or many bright colors.

Form four large cones from colored paper to use as decorations for the bag. Cut four sets of crepe paper or tissue paper streamers to form tassels for the ends of the cones. Glue or tape them to the points of the cones. Tape one cone to each of the four sides of the bag. Add long streamers to the bottom of the bag.

To play the game, tie the *piñata* to a broom handle. Have someone tall hold it above the heads of the players. Blindfold each person in turn, give him or her a stick, and direct the player to take three tries to attempt to break the *piñata* while it is being raised and lowered by the person holding the broom. When the bag breaks the children may gather the goodies.*

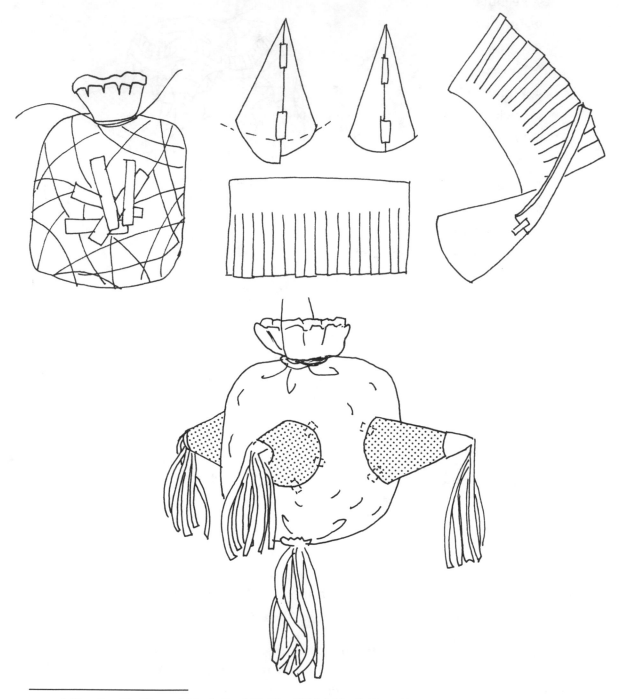

* Fiarotta, Phyllis and Noel. *Confetti: The Kids' Make-It-Yourself, Do-It-Yourself Party Book*. New York: Workman, 1978.

•NETHERLANDS•

Country Information

*F*ifteen million people inhabit the Kingdom of the Netherlands. The population is predominately Dutch with some Moroccan, Turk, Indonesian, and Surinamese people as well. Roman Catholic and Protestant, especially the Dutch Reformed church, of which the Queen is a member, are the main religions.

The Netherlands is bordered by the North Sea, Belgium, and Germany. The country is low and flat. Because much of the area is below sea level, the Dutch have had to build their famous dikes to reclaim land from the sea.

The country is often called Holland, the name of the two largest Dutch provinces (North Holland and South Holland), which include the country's three largest and most prosperous cities: Amsterdam, the capital of the Netherlands, The Hague, and Rotterdam.

Natural gas is the country's greatest resource. Agricultural products include wheat, barley, oats, sugar beets, fruits, potatoes, poultry, vegetables, flowers, and bulbs. Petroleum refining, steel, metal products, electronics, ship building, bulk chemicals, and natural gas are some of the industries found in the Netherlands.*

---

* Holly, Susan, Editor. *Background Notes: Netherlands*. Washington, DC: United States Department of State, 1991.

Flag

Three horizontal stripes, red, white, and blue, from top to bottom, form the field of the flag of the Netherlands.

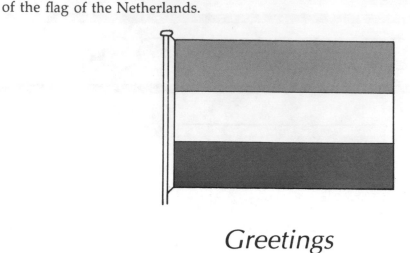

Greetings

The official language of the Netherlands is Dutch. The Christmas greeting is *Zalig Kerstfeest*. The greeting of peace is *Vrede*.

Customs

Festivities, food, faith, and family highlight the celebration of Christmas in the Netherlands. On a Saturday in mid-November a steamer from Spain arrives in the harbor bringing Saint Nicholas, his horse, and Black Pete to Holland. They come several weeks before December 6 to make preparations for the celebrations that will take place on Saint Nicholas Day.

Before the children go to bed on December 5 they fill their shoes with carrots and hay for Saint Nicholas' horse. In the morning the shoes contain candy, fruit, and small gifts.

Christmas trees are often bought off of barges in the canals, taken home, and trimmed with ornaments and candles. Houses are also decorated with pine, holly, and flowers.

Traditionally, inexpensive gifts are exchanged on Saint Nicholas Eve or Christmas Eve. Each present, accompanied by an original verse, is disguised in an amusing wrapping.

Christmas Eve or Christmas morning, and often both times, includes attendance at a church service. The first Christmas Day, December 25, is spent with family and friends. Gifts such as books may be exchanged in the morning, and visiting takes place in the afternoon. Early in the evening an elaborate dinner is served.

On the second Christmas Day, December 26, family and friends often dine out and attend concerts. Nearly all Dutch music societies, professional vocalists, school choirs, and amateur groups participate in performances in auditoriums, concert halls, and churches.

Crèche

The nativity scene has a prominent place in the homes and the hearts of the people of Holland. Called the *Kerststal*, the crèche is placed near or under the family Christmas tree.

Throughout the ages, Dutch painters have depicted scenes from the Christmas story in many ways. Various materials and methods have been used to illustrate the Annunciation, Madonna and Child, Holy Family, Adoration of the Shepherds, Presentation in the Temple, and Visit of the Magi.

During the Christmas season explore several ways in which artists of the Netherlands have represented the nativity story. Observe paintings such as these by the famous Dutch artist Rembrandt:

"The Adoration of the Shepherds"
"The Holy Family"
"The Presentation in the Temple"
"Simeon in the Temple"

To explore the world of painting by the masters, choose one or more of the following possibilities:

- Visit an art museum and view the collection of paintings and other art.
- Tour a church and discover its Advent and Christmas art.
- Look in art books for reproductions of well-known paintings.
- Page through books on periods of art such as the Middle Ages, Renaissance, and others.
- Find information in encyclopedias.
- Read biographies of artists.
- Look at pictures in Bibles and bible story books.
- Discover drawings in prayer books.
- Complete pictures in specialized coloring books.
- View slides.
- Watch a film or video about paintings and painters.
- Notice the art on:
  - Christmas cards
  - Note cards and stationery
  - Postcards
  - Posters
  - Postage stamps
  - Commemorative plates

You might also look at other media such as stained glass, tapestries, sculpture, mosaics, vestments, altar pieces, and medallions. *

---

* Wezeman, Phyllis Vos and Jude Dennis Fournier. "Art Approaches." *Counting the Days: Twenty-Five Ways.* Brea, CA: Educational Ministries, Inc., 1989, pp. 7–8.

Gift Giver

In the Netherlands Christmas festivities begin on the eve of December 6, Saint Nicholas Day. Saint Nicholas, also called *Sinterklaas*, the gift giver of the Dutch people, was born in Asia Minor in the fourth century. When his wealthy parents died in an epidemic, he traded his luxury for a life of doing good deeds and gave all of his money to the poor. Nicholas devoted himself to prayer, became a priest, and was made bishop of Myra while still a young man. Within a century of his death he was named a saint and is considered the patron saint of children, sailors, and merchants. December 6, the anniversary of his death, is a joyous occasion for gift giving in the country of Holland.

Saint Nicholas arrives in the Netherlands on a steamer that carries him from Spain. He wears the vestments of a bishop, but the holiday is without religious overtones. The white haired, white bearded man generally wears a white robe with a crimson mantel. His headdress is a tall red miter and he carries a golden crosier, a staff shaped like a shepherd's crook. Saint Nicholas rides a white horse as he parades through town and travels from rooftop to rooftop visiting every home.

Accompanying Saint Nicholas is *Zwarte Piet*, or Black Pete, a Moor dressed like a sixteenth-century Spanish page. Pete is frivolous and jolly and carries a big red book in which *Sinterklaas* has kept a record all year of the children's behavior. Pete also brings birch rods, or switches, to use to punish naughty children. His big bag contains fruits, chocolates, and cookies for good boys and girls.

Before Dutch children go to bed on December 5 they fill their shoes with carrots, hay, and snacks for Saint Nicholas' horse and leave them near the hearth or the kitchen stove. During the night it is said that Pete descends the chimney to get the snack and fills the shoes with candy, fruit, and small gifts such as yo-yos, paper, and pencils. Sometimes there is a knock on the door and Pete's hand throws candy and cookies in the hall or leaves a basket of gifts.

Card

Exchanging holiday greetings between immediate family and close friends is a fun-filled custom in the Netherlands. Much imagination and ingenuity accompany the tradition. It is customary to attach a card, containing an original verse, to a small gift that has been disguised in some unusual or amusing wrapping. The humorous verse on the card gently teases the person who receives it. Department stores employ "*Sneldichters*" (fast poets) during the holiday season who can be hired to write verses for shoppers. Regardless of who writes the poetry, all cards are signed by Saint Nicholas or Black Pete.

Create a Christmas card that combines a collage of Dutch holiday scenes and an original verse and give it to someone special.

Materials:

- ✧ Construction paper
- ✧ Glue
- ✧ Markers
- ✧ Scissors
- ✧ Magazines
- ✧ Scraps of tissue paper, paper doilies, and woodgrain contact paper

Method:

Fold the construction paper in half to form a card. The collage will be glued to the cover and the verse will be written inside.

Plan the design of the collage. Include pictures of customs and traditions associated with the Christmas season in the Netherlands, such as Saint Nicholas, churches, families, foods, musicians, and skaters. Cut the illustrations from magazines and brochures. Make items for which pictures cannot be found from a variety of other materials. Ideas include using woodgrain contact paper for wooden shoes, paper doilies for lace tablecloths or curtains, and foil paper for candle holders and ornaments. Arrange the collage attractively on the paper and glue the pieces in place.

Compose a verse for the inside of the card. It could explain this Dutch custom or it might be a humorous stanza teasing the person who will receive it. Here's a sample:

In the country of the Dutch
They celebrate Christmas with a special touch.
Each card is written in a way that's fun,
And given with a gift to a special one.

Crafts

—■—

Since windmills are a common sight throughout the Netherlands, paper pinwheels are popular decorations on Christmas trees in Dutch homes. Follow the easy directions below to make pinwheels in different colors and sizes, and from various types of paper. To use them as toys for children, attach a straw for a handle rather than a pipe cleaner for a hanger.

Ceramic tiles painted with blue and white designs have been used in Dutch homes for decorative and utilitarian purposes for centuries. Simple patterns often enhance a single tile and elaborate themes can cover an entire wall of ceramic pieces.

Try painting a tile to use as a holiday decoration or to give as a unique gift. Make up several small tiles as Christmas tree ornaments. Purchase white glazed ceramic tiles from floor covering centers.

Paper Pinwheels

Materials:

      ✧ Two-color craft or foil paper   ✧ Glue

      ✧ Scissors   ✧ 1″ brass fasteners

      ✧ Ruler   ✧ Pipe cleaners

      ✧ Pencil

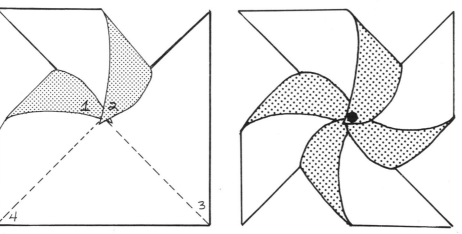

Method:

For each pinwheel, measure and cut a six inch square from two-colored craft paper. If this type of paper is not available, use two different colors of construction paper and glue two squares together.

Fold the square in half diagonally and crease it. Open the paper and fold it diagonally to the opposite corners. Re-open the square. Draw a one inch circle in the center of the paper. Cut each folded line from the corner to the edge of the circle. One by one, bring the right corner of each triangle to the center of the square, bending each piece over the previous section.

Make a small hole in the center of the four points and push a paper fastener through the front of it. Open the fastener at the back of the pinwheel. Attach a pipe cleaner to the back of the fastener and use the loop to hang the ornament on the tree.

Ceramic Tiles

Materials:

- ◇ Ceramic tiles
- ◇ Acrylic paint, blue
- ◇ Brushes
- ◇ Paper
- ◇ Pencils

Method:

Begin by brainstorming a list of designs that might be found on Dutch tiles. Include windmills, wooden shoes, tulips, ships, canals, harbors, fruits, and vegetables. Choose one theme to use on each tile. Practice drawing it on a piece of paper before painting it on the ceramic. To make the project more authentic, each corner of the tile should contain a design such as a flower or a heart.

Using pencil, draw the sketch on the tile. Carefully fill in the motif with blue paint. Since the paint will chip off easily with this method, allow it to dry thoroughly and handle the tile with care.

Carols

___ ■ ___

Music plays an important part in the celebration of Christmas in the Netherlands. Two Dutch carols are "Come and Stand Amazed, You People" and "The Garden of Jesus."

Story

A Day to Remember by Bernard Stone (New York: Four Winds Press, 1981) depicts the activities of a nineteenth-century Dutch town as it prepares for the feast of Saint Nicholas and Christmas Day.

Culinary

Dutch delicacies abound in stores and homes in the Netherlands during the season of Christmas. *Borstplaat*, a hard, smooth fondant sugar candy; *pepernoten*, a type of cookie; marzipan, almond paste shaped into clever animals, fruits, and vegetables; and chocolate wooden shoes are among the favorites. *Speculaas*, or windmill cookies, are often formed in wooden molds. One holiday tradition is *banket*, a flaky pastry filled with almond paste, and sometimes shaped into the initials of people's names.

The noon meal on Christmas Day is called *Koffietafel*, or coffee table, and is more like a huge breakfast. Early in the evening, around seven o'clock, a dinner of ham and traditional favorites is served. The Christmas story is read from the Bible.

Recipes for *banket* and for *speculaas* are provided.

Banket

Flaky pastry is filled with almond paste and baked into long strips or into the shape of initials of people's names. It is a great treat for every child in the family to receive his or her own *banket* letter as a gift.

Ingredients:

- ✧ 4 cups unsifted flour
- ✧ 1 pound margarine
- ✧ l cup cold water
- ✧ 4 cups almond paste, grated
- ✧ 4 eggs
- ✧ 2 cups sugar
- ✧ 1 teaspoon vanilla

Method:

Cut the margarine into the flour until the mixture resembles cornmeal. Add the water and stir to form a smooth dough. Place the crust in the refrigerator overnight.

Prepare the filling by mixing four cups grated almond paste, three eggs and the yolk of the fourth egg, sugar, and vanilla. Save the other egg white for the top of the strips.

Cut the dough into eight pieces. Roll each of them into a long strip. Place filling down the center of each piece and roll up the ends and the sides of the dough. To form an initial, gently shape and combine the strips into the desired letter. Brush the top of each strip with unbeaten egg white. Cut a small slash every inch or two into the tops of the strips.

Bake in a 450 degree oven for twelve to fifteen minutes, or until golden brown. Makes eight strips. To serve, cut the strips into two inch pieces.

Speculaas

This traditional Christmas cookie is similar to gingerbread and may come in many shapes, including windmills.

Ingredients:

- ❖ 1 cup unsalted butter, softened
- ❖ 2 teaspoons vanilla
- ❖ 1 1/4 cups dark brown sugar, firmly packed
- ❖ 1 cup white sugar
- ❖ 2 large eggs, beaten
- ❖ 3 1/2 cups all-purpose flour
- ❖ 2 teaspoons baking soda
- ❖ 2 teaspoons cinnamon
- ❖ 1 teaspoon nutmeg
- ❖ 1 teaspoon ground cloves
- ❖ 1/2 teaspoon ginger
- ❖ 1/2 teaspoon ground anise seed
- ❖ 1/8 teaspoon salt

Method:

Combine the butter, sugars, and vanilla and beat until light and fluffy. Add the beaten eggs and blend well.

Sift the flour together with the dry ingredients and beat into the butter mixture.

Roll small pieces of dough into balls and place them on a greased cookie sheet. Bake for ten to fifteen minutes in a 350 degree oven. Makes about sixty small cookies.

Game

Weather permitting, Dutch families and friends like to go ice skating on Christmas Day. In the winter, when the canals freeze over, skating is the most popular sport in the country.

Families also enjoy spending the holidays doing puzzles and playing board games. Make up a game of concentration and use it to review some of the Christmas customs of the Netherlands.

Materials:

- ✦ Index cards
- ✦ Markers or crayons

Method:

Brainstorm a list of Dutch holiday traditions. It could include:

- ✦ Ice skating
- ✦ Banket letters
- ✦ Marzipan candies
- ✦ Church services
- ✦ Pinwheels
- ✦ Wooden shoes
- ✦ Saint Nicholas

Try to think of at least ten to twelve things to use for the game.

Prepare two index cards for each tradition. Write the same word or draw the same picture of the item on each of the cards. Make as many sets as desired.

To play the game, mix up the index cards and place them face down on a table or on the floor. Instruct the first player to turn two cards face up. If they match, the person takes another turn. If the cards do not match, they are turned face down again and the next person takes a turn. Play continues until all of the cards have been matched.

▪NIGERIA▪

Country Information

One hundred nineteen million people live in Nigeria, Africa's most populous country. The inhabitants represent two hundred and fifty tribal groups, the largest of which are Hausa-Fulani, Ibo, and Yoruba. English is the official language, but most people also speak one or two native dialects. Only twenty-five percent of the Nigerian population lives in urban areas, and these people have modern education, health, and commerce practices. Most of the people are farmers and reside in country regions where traditional customs are still observed. Religions in Nigeria include Islam, Christianity, and indigenous African religions.

Nigeria is located on the west coast of the African continent. It is bounded on the south by the Gulf of Guinea, on the east by Cameroon and Chad, on the north by Niger, and on the west by Benin. The country covers an area more than twice the size of California.

Nigeria's terrain ranges from southern coastal swamps to tropical forests, open woodlands, grasslands, and semi-desert. Two seasons, dry and wet, are well marked throughout most of Nigeria. The country has several navigable rivers, the Niger, the Benue, and the Cross, which play an important role in transportation and economic activity.

Nigeria's natural resources include petroleum, tin, columbite, iron ore, coal, limestone, lead, and zinc. The oil boom of the 1970s shifted Nigeria from an agriculturally based economy to one that relies on oil for most of its export earnings and federal budget revenues. While this has had a devastating impact on agriculture, products most frequently produced are cocoa, palm oil, yams, cassava, sorghum, millet, corn, rice, livestock, groundnuts, and cotton. Leading industries vary from textiles, cement, and food products, to footwear, metal products, and lumber.*

Flag

Nigeria's flag is composed of green, white, and green vertical bands.

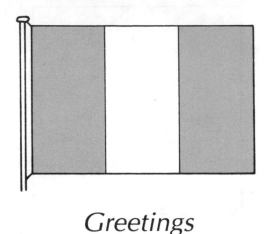

Greetings

The predominant languages of Nigeria include English, Hausa, Ibo, and Yoruba. The Christmas greeting is *Merry Christmas*, and the greeting of peace is *peace*. However, *Yesu yana Kaunacce ni* (yay'-su yah'nah Kow'-nah-chay' Knee), or Jesus Loves Me, is the message in Hausa that is proclaimed by young and old during the Christmas season.

Customs

Approximately forty percent of the one hundred fifteen million inhabitants of this west African nation are Christians. The birthday of the Savior is an occasion for great joy and celebration.

It is customary for Nigerians to wear new clothes on Christmas. For men and boys it could be shirts and trousers, or robes and hats, while women generally wear a blouse and body wrap of colorful fabric and a brightly patterned head tie.

Church services on Christmas involve large pageants with many scenes. The long, elaborate productions, with many actors and actresses, last for several hours. No scripts are used and the lines are ad-libbed. Worship services and programs provide wonderful ways to celebrate the gospel story and to share the good news

---

* Holly, Susan, Editor. *Background Notes: Nigeria*. Washington, DC: United States Department of State, 1991.

with non-Christian relatives and friends, many of whom practice Islam or tribal religions.

Although giving gifts is not as popular in Nigeria as it is in the United States, people tend to go from house to house, similar to trick or treating, in the hopes of getting candy or coins.

Singing and dancing are part of all festive occasions in Africa, and Christmas is no exception. On Christmas afternoon dances begin near the chief's compound and continue long into the night. All people in the village participate.

Crèche

Ceremonial masks are a very important part of Nigerian celebrations. These works of art frequently represent important people from the African culture. Often a calabash (a gourd-like plant) is decorated as a mask or made into a musical instrument.

Make a set of papier-mâché masks and use them to tell the Christmas story.

Materials:

- ✧ Newspaper
- ✧ Scissors
- ✧ Glue (white)
- ✧ Water
- ✧ Container or bucket
- ✧ Paint stirrer

- ✧ Balloons
- ✧ Paint
- ✧ Brushes
- ✧ Shellac
- ✧ Trims
- ✧ Bible

Method:

Make a ceremonial mask for each person from the nativity story. Include Mary, Joseph, the baby Jesus, and perhaps the three kings and the shepherds. Masks might also be made to represent the manger animals.

Cut or tear newspaper into one inch strips. Combine white glue and water in a large container or bucket and stir until it is completely mixed. For each character, inflate a large round balloon. Dip a strip of newspaper into the glue and water solution and stick it to the balloon. Continue this process until one half of the balloon is completely covered. Repeat the procedure until the mask has four to five layers of newspaper strips. Allow the pieces to dry completely, preferably overnight. Remove the balloons from the open ends of the papier-mâché masks.

Paint the masks with bright colors. Add facial features to represent the various people from the Christmas story. After the masks are painted, give each of them a coat of shellac to serve as a sealant. Add special features with yarn, feathers, raffia, crepe paper, beads, and other trims. The decorative touches will create authentic looking masks.

Once the character faces are completed have someone read the Christmas story from the Bible and act out the passage using the ceremonial masks. Also try using the face pieces to illustrate the words of the African American Christmas carol, "Go Tell It on the Mountain."

Gift Giver

— ■ —

In many ways, we could say that Christian missionaries are the gift givers in Nigeria. The Christmas story itself is a new gift to the people of Nigeria. Christmas becomes a time to share the story of the Messiah with others. Because the church in Nigeria is very young, fervent prayer is greatly needed for these people. Use this service to pray for our Nigerian brothers and sisters and for all those who give the Christian stories to these people.

Prayer Service

Materials:

- ✧ Table
- ✧ Cloth, African fabric if possible
- ✧ Candle
- ✧ Basket
- ✧ Incense
- ✧ Incense container

- ✧ Matches
- ✧ Bible
- ✧ Pencils
- ✧ Paper
- ✧ Music for selected songs
- ✧ Accompaniment

Advance Preparation:

Set up a worship center by covering the table with a piece of African cloth. Place the candle, empty basket, paper, pencils, incense and container, matches, and open Bible on it.

Select two readers to participate in the service.

Opening Song: "Go, Tell It on the Mountain"

Opening Prayer

Leader: Redeemer God, you who give strength to those who believe, give to us now the strength and courage to tell the good news of Jesus' birth.

Help us to be fervent in word and belief as we share your love with all of humankind. Jesus was born in simple surroundings and in a humble home. May his life be an example for all the world and a light in our eyes.

Bless us now as we gather to pray and celebrate the coming of Christ in our world.

All: Amen.

Reading

Adapted from John 1

One: In the beginning was the Word;
The Word was in God's presence,
And the Word was God.
The Word was present to God in the beginning.
Through the Word all things came into being,
And apart from the Word nothing came to be.
Whatever came to be in the Word, found life,
Life for the light of all nations.
The light shines on in darkness, a darkness that did not overcome it.

Two: There was a man named John sent by God who came as a witness to testify to the Word, so that through him all people might believe — but only to testify to the light, for he himself was not the light. The real light which gives light to every person was coming into the world.

Readers One and Two:

The Word became flesh
And made a dwelling among us,
And we have seen the glory:
The glory of Jesus coming from the heavens
Filled with enduring love.

Scripture Sharing

Leader: Silently reflect on the scripture reading. After a few moments think about what word or words you would share about the person of Jesus Christ. What word would you use to describe this man? What would you say if the people you were speaking to knew nothing about him? What gift would you want to leave with them?

You are invited to use the slips of paper and pencils that are being passed out to write down some of your reflections. Write an answer to one of the questions.

As the basket is passed through the community, place your slips of paper into it. The basket will be placed in the center of the prayer table. It will be incensed as a sign of our commitment to share the good word of the news of Jesus' coming with other people.

Closing

Leader: Let us pray for the needs of all people:

For women, men, and children who are just now hearing the good news, that the word will live and grow deep within.

For those people who have not heard, that their hearts will soon hold the power of the Spirit.

For all women and men who dare to go where sharing the word will cause insults and hate toward them. May they find strength to journey on.

For young people, that they may believe.

Please share your own prayers at this time.

Let us all join hands and share together "The Lord's Prayer."

Now let us offer to one another a word of love and peace.

Closing song: "Rise Up, Shepherd, and Follow"

Card

In Nigeria, as well as other African nations, beautiful designs are created by stamping interesting shapes and textures onto cloth and other materials. Some of the designs tell stories or have religious significance, while others are simply works of art. Make a unique Christmas card by using a modified version of this stamping technique.

Materials:

- ✧ Liquid tempera paint or finger paint
- ✧ Shallow pans
- ✧ Cylinders such as rolling pins, juice cans, pop cans, spools, cardboard tubes
- ✧ Yarn
- ✧ String
- ✧ Glue
- ✧ Scissors
- ✧ Posterboard
- ✧ Sponge
- ✧ Paper
- ✧ Paper towels
- ✧ Newspaper

Method:

Printing a design on a card to use during the twelve days of Christmas is a fun and festive way to experience one of the art forms of Africa. A simple way to create the "stamps" is to form various designs on cylinders and roll them across paper.

Select a piece of paper to use for the card. Decide on the designs that will be formed on it. Suggestions are to glue yarn or string in a pattern on a juice can, wrap string or cord around a tube, or cut shapes from posterboard or sponge and attach them to a pop can.

Pour each color of paint into a shallow container. Roll the tube in the paint. Roll the cylinder across the paper. This may be done several times to create a repeated pattern. Allow the paint to dry.

Fold the card in half, and write a holiday message on the inside of it. Send or give the card as a special greeting of the season.

This technique may be used to make wrapping paper too.

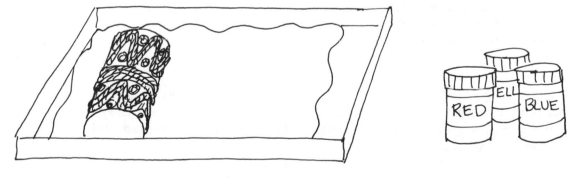

Crafts

Arts and crafts associated with Nigeria are closely tied in with ceremony, tradition, and tribal custom. Great diversity exists among Nigeria's numerous cultures. The two craft projects below provide an opportunity to create in a traditional African spirit.

Tie-Dye T-Shirts

Tie-dye is a traditional art in many countries of west Africa including Nigeria. Designs are created on cloth by folding, bunching, or twisting material and binding it very tightly so that the bound areas will resist penetration of color when the material is immersed into a dye bath. Tie-dyed fabrics are used by African men, women, and children as wrap-around skirts, robes, shirts, and head pieces. Try making a unique T-shirt by using this technique.

Materials:

- T-shirts
- Dye, non-toxic
- Water
- Salt
- Measuring spoon
- Rubber bands, small
- String or cord, various thicknesses
- Scissors
- Kettles or dishpans
- Tongs, large spoon, or stick
- Newspaper
- Plastic table covering
- Clothesline or rack
- Clip clothespins
- Paper towels or rags
- Buttons, beads, seeds, marbles
- Iron

Method:

Prepare different colors of dye in separate kettles or dishpans. Use standard dye, specially formulated cold water dye, Kool-Aid, or natural dye from berries and plants. Make strong colors by using less water than indicated on the package. Add salt, approximately one tablespoon per batch, to make the dye more colorfast.

Choose a T-shirt to use for the project. One that is mostly cotton will absorb the dyes better than cloth that is synthetic. Assemble a variety of rubber bands, string, and cord. Gather up small tufts of material and tightly bind them with rubber bands or firmly tie them with pieces of string or cord. Note that different thicknesses of cord and string will result in varied patterns. Plastic-coated twist ties or pipe cleaners may also be used to tie the cloth.

Placing objects such as beads, buttons, stones, or seeds into tied or bound areas will result in interesting patterns and textures on the shirt. Tying the cloth around marbles or beans makes small circles. Folding accordian style and tying makes different linear patterns.

The next step is to dip the cloth into dye. Immerse the tied cloth into a dye pot. Allow time for the fabric to absorb the liquid. Use tongs, a large spoon, or a stick to swish the cloth around and to lift the dyed article from the container. Leave the material in the dye until it is a shade darker than desired as it will dry to a lighter hue. The fabric may be dipped in second and third dyes while still wet to create blended colors. Just tufts may be dipped into dye instead of immersing the whole piece.

Remove the wet fabric to a covered work space or to a clothesline to dry. When the T-shirt is dry, use sharp pointed scissors and carefully clip the rubber bands and cords. These should be discarded. Dried fabric may be retied and dipped in a different color. If this is done, repeat the procedure and the drying process.

The finished piece may be ironed or just stretched and smoothed to show the designs.

Beaded Pins

African artisans use beads to create headbands, armbands, necklaces, costume adornments, dolls, and house decorations. The cheerful, colorful designs often symbolize a story or religious message. Although the elaborate beaded decorations are generally reserved for special occasions, children often wear a beaded safety pin or bead decoration on a blouse, shirt, or sweater. These are sometimes referred to as friendship pins. Try making several of them to wear and to give as Christmas gifts.

Materials:

    ◇ Colored beads with holes   ◇ Safety pins (large)

Method:

Gather a variety of colored beads or buy them at a craft store. The beads should be small, but the holes need to be large enough to thread onto the pin.

Thread a few beads on a pin in an attractive pattern. Make a variety of beaded pins to keep or to give away.

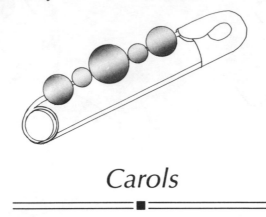

Carols

Christmas afternoon is a time when Nigerian children go caroling at the homes of their wealthier neighbors. Some young people wear masks and anticipate receiving candy and cookies in exchange for their songs.

Two Christmas carols that have come to us from the African American culture are "Go, Tell It on the Mountain" and "Rise Up, Shepherd, and Follow." These would be an appropriate way to celebrate Christmas in the Nigerian spirit.

Story

Music and musical instruments are important parts of Nigerian celebrations and feast days. The drum, often called the heartbeat of the continent, is considered to be the most significant instrument. It is said that a Nigerian baby is born to the sound of the drums. This makes the drum an appropriate instrument to use to proclaim the birth of the baby who came to be the Savior of the world.

Group rhythm patterns add a lively dimension to storytelling in this African country. Certain sounds heighten the drama of each scene. A constant drum beat with intermittent rhythm instruments may be used to show the importance of the story being told.

Although the Christmas story is relatively new to the country of Nigeria, it is extremely precious to the Christians of the nation. Construct handmade drums and rhythm instruments and use them to enhance and illustrate the importance of the Christmas story.

Materials:

⋄ Coffee cans or plastic tubs with lids   ⋄ Rocks and pebbles
⋄ Canvas   ⋄ Pop top cans
⋄ String   ⋄ Soup cans

- ✧ Pencils or dowel rods
- ✧ Felt
- ✧ Rubber bands
- ✧ Band aid boxes
- ✧ Fabric
- ✧ Scissors
- ✧ Bible

Method:

Simple drums can be made out of coffee cans and margarine or peanut butter tubs with lids. Turn large cans or oatmeal cartons into drums by stretching canvas over the top of them. Secure the material in place with rope or rubber bands. Make drumsticks by wrapping felt around the ends of pencils or dowel rods and putting rubber bands around the fabric.

Shakers would be good rhythm instruments to use in storytelling. Create them by putting rocks or pebbles into band-aid boxes or by placing pop tops in soup cans. Cover the open end with fabric held in place with rubber bands.

After the drums and shakers are constructed, ask the participants to form a circle. Provide each person with a musical instrument. Choose a storyteller and ask this person to stand in the center of the group and to read the Christmas story from the Bible. Once the narrator starts, the drums should begin sounding. As the storyteller nears the part of the passage announcing the birth of Jesus, the shakers and any other instruments should be played. The circle could move slowly to the right during the telling of the story.

Culinary

"Christmas day in Jos, Nigeria, begins with a neighborhood food exchange. People prepare large pots of chicken stew and rice in advance. Then on Christmas morning, neighbors begin sending bowls of chicken stew and rice to each other.

"In the afternoon women go dancing and singing from house to house, and people stop to visit. Each family has a large pot of a traditional grain drink prepared to serve their guests. They also serve meat, rice, and sweets on this occasion. Food is a symbol of joyful sharing."*

---

* Schlabach, Joetta Handrich. *Extending the Table. . . A World Community Cookbook.* Scottdale, PA: Herald Press, 1991, p. 313. Used by permission.

Sesame Seed Cookies

Add to the holiday festivities by cutting the dough for these sweet, crunchy cookies into a variety of seasonal shapes.

Ingredients:

- 3/4 cup shortening or margarine
- 1 cup sugar
- 1 teaspoon vanilla
  or 1/2 teaspoon lemon extract
- 2 1/2 cups flour
- 1 teaspoon baking powder
- 1 teaspoon salt
- 1 cup sesame seeds

Method:

Cream together the shortening or margarine, sugar, eggs, and flavoring. Add the flour, baking powder, salt, and sesame seeds. Stir until well blended. Cover and chill at least one hour. Preheat oven to 400 degrees. Roll dough 1/8 inch thick on lightly floured, cloth-covered board. Cut into desired shapes. Place on ungreased baking sheets. Bake eight to ten minutes or until very light brown.*

Nigerian Meat Soup

Chicken, beef, or another type of meat may be included in this recipe.

Ingredients:

- 1/4 cup oil
- 1 pound meat, cubed
- 2 cups water
- 1 onion, chopped
- 1 small can tomato paste
- Red pepper or Tobasco sauce to taste
- Salt
- Rice

Method:

Brown the meat in the oil. Add one cup water and simmer forty-five minutes or until tender. If chicken is used, cut it into pieces and cook them in the water until tender. Add tomato paste, onion, pepper, salt, and remaining water. Cover and simmer twenty-five minutes.

Serve the soup over rice.

Game

Nigeria is a country rich with music, stories, celebrations, and rituals. Many customs and special activities are used to help ritualize the ceremonies and holidays of this African nation.

---

* *Ibid.*, p. 313. Used by permission.

Review all that has been learned about the celebration of Christmas in Nigeria. Play a word game to help remember the many customs. Choose a word associated with the season, for example "drum." Draw a line for each letter of the word. The object is for the players to fill in the letters of the selected word from a series of clue words. Write a clue for each letter of the keyword by picking words which contain these letters. To illustrate, the clue word for the "d" of drum might be band. Leave off the "d" of the clue and write 1. ban___. Have the participants guess the letter and fill it in. They must then write that letter in the corresponding square of the mystery word.

Start with the words provided, and make up several more. They may be written on paper or on a chalkboard.

___   ___   ___   ___

 1   2   3   4

1. ban___

2. a___m

3. p___mp

4. ___usic

(D R U M)

___   ___   ___ - ___   ___   ___   ___   ___   ___

 1   2   3   4   5   6   7   8   9

1. ca___

2. b___te

3. m___at

4. ___ark

5. ___arn

6. ___ye

7. m___ce

8. ___ose

9. ___ive

(T I E-D Y E I N G)

—   —   —   —   —   —   —
1   2   3   4   5   6   7

1. t__n

2. __east

3. __ice

4. f__t

5. __ar

6. co__l

7. __ot

(AFRICAN)

▪POLAND▪

Country Information

▬▬▬▬▬▬ ▪ ▬▬▬▬▬▬

*P*oland, a country the size of the state of New Mexico, is located in Eastern Europe. Its natural boundries are the Baltic Sea on the north and the Carpathian Mountains on the south along the border it shares with Czechoslovakia. To the east and west, the country is part of a continuous plain that starts in central Europe and continues to the Ural Mountains. The climate is temperate, with moderately severe winters and mild summers.

The country's thirty-eight million inhabitants are nearly ninety-nine percent ethnic Poles. The remaining residents are mostly Byelorussian or Ukrainian. Most Polish people are Roman Catholic and the remainder belong mainly to the Eastern Orthodox or Protestant religions.

The Republic of Poland is Eastern Europe's leading producer of potatoes, cannola, sugar beets, grains, hogs, and cattle. Poland's industrial base has expanded beyond coal, textiles, chemicals, machinery, iron, and steel. It now includes newly developed industries such as fertilizers, petrochemicals, machine tools, electrical machinery, electronics, and ship building.*

―――――――――

* Young, Phyllis, Editor. *Background Notes: Poland*. Washington, DC: United States Department of State, 1991.

Flag

Two horizontal bands, upper white and lower red, make up the field of Poland's flag. An eagle centered in a red square appears in the middle of the white strip.

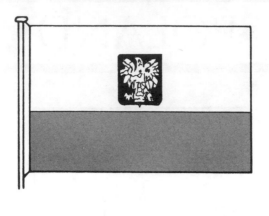

Greetings

The Christmas greeting in Polish is *Wesolych Swiat*. The greeting of peace is *Pokoj*.

Customs

Christmas in Poland is celebrated with religious ceremonies and rich folk traditions that form the bond between the country's past and present. Holiday preparations begin four weeks before Christmas, the start of the season of Advent, and festivities continue through January 6 or February 2. The cycle includes a number of feast days in honor of various saints, and each of them has its own religious observances, folk customs, and special meals.

Centuries ago Advent was observed for forty days, like Lent, and began November 11 on the Feast of Saint Martin. Currently, early activities center around Saint Catherine's Day, November 25, and Saint Andrew's Day, November 30. Often the games played by young men and women are filled with romantic prophecies and fortune telling.

The Christmas tree, or *choinka*, can be trimmed any time during Advent, although traditionally it is decorated during the afternoon of *Wigilia*, December 24. The custom of the tree is a recent tradition. Previously *pajaki*, handmade mobiles, were suspended from the ceiling. These wreaths were constructed from the best grains of the previous summer and decorated with nuts, apples, and paper cut-outs. Next came the custom of suspending the top of a fir tree upside down from the ceiling. It, too, was lavishly laden with apples, nuts, candies, and small toys.

The entire family is involved in preparing handmade ornaments for the tree. Most are crafted from paper and other readily available materials. Eggs, symbolizing the miracle of birth, are often blown out, decorated, and hung on the tree.

On Christmas Eve the *Wigilia* supper takes place. After this meal the entire family attends the midnight mass of the shepherds. Festivities and feasts take place at the homes of family and friends following the service.

Christmas Day, December 25, is celebrated with family; it begins *Gody*, the twelve days of Christmas. Three masses are offered that day and each has different prayers and scripture readings.

Saint Stephen's Day, December 26, is celebrated with friends and extended family members. *Szopki*, or puppet, plays are presented. Carols, which fall into the three categories of legendary (apocryphal), religious, and pastoral (shepherd's songs), are sung. Two more feast days during the Christmas season are the Feast of Saint John the Apostle on December 27 and Saint Sylvester's Day, also called the Feast of the Circumcision of our Lord, on January 1.

In many regions Epiphany, the Feast of the Three Kings, on January 6, marks the end of the Christmas season. It is observed with a service of blessing of the home. In other areas of Poland, especially the rural ones, the season of Christmas concludes on the feast of the Purification of our Lady, February 2.

Crèche

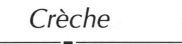

Szopki, or nativity scenes, were first displayed in churches in Poland in the fourteenth century. Soon the figures in the exhibit were used by the parishioners to present religious theatrical performances. Each year, new characters and events were added and over the centuries the *szopka* play presented a picture of Polish life as well as the story of the birth of the babe in Bethlehem. Today puppet plays depicting the nativity story are performed in Polish cities, towns, and villages throughout the season of Christmas. The *szopka* may be a small box decorated to represent a stable or it can be an elaborate structure of a church or cathedral complete with domes, towers, arcades, columns, and galleries. During the Christmas season Polish children carry the *szopka* from house to house, singing carols and presenting puppet shows. Families watch the plays and give the children small gifts of money.

Construct a simple *szopka* and a set of paper puppets to tell the Christmas story in this traditional Polish manner.

Materials:

- ✧ Cardboard carton
- ✧ Cardboard pieces
- ✧ Posterboard
- ✧ Colored and metallic papers
- ✧ Scissors
- ✧ Glue
- ✧ X-acto knife
- ✧ Poster paints, various colors
- ✧ Brushes
- ✧ Craft sticks
- ✧ Magazines or church school papers
- ✧ Table
- ✧ Cloth or sheet

Method:

Using an X-acto knife, cut a hole in the center of the bottom of a carton. Leave a three to five inch border around the opening to add support to the stage.

Decorate the box to represent an elaborate church. Polish people often copy the style of their own churches and make them even more elaborate and colorful than in reality. In this way they identify more closely with the Christmas story.

Cut two identical tower shapes from cardboard or posterboard and glue them to the right and left sides of the stage. Cut a dome for the center portion of the box. Glue it in place above the stage opening.

Embellish the *szopka* with paint and paper. Use poster paints and brightly colored, as well as silver and gold, paper to decorate the stage with stained glass windows, balconies, stars, crosses, angels, and other designs.

Set the stage aside and form simple paper puppets to use to present the nativity story. Draw the characters of the Christmas story on posterboard and cut them out. An alternative method is to make the puppets by cutting the figures from church school papers, magazines, greeting cards, or coloring books. Back these puppets with posterboard. Glue a craft stick to the back of each figure. Make sure at least half of the stick extends below the bottom of the character. This is the rod by which the puppet is operated.

Drape a cloth over a table and set the *szopka* on top of it. Kneel behind the table and the stage and use the rod puppets to present the nativity story through the opening in the box.

Gift Giver

Children in Poland receive their first Christmas gifts on Saint Nicholas Day, December 6. The kindly gentleman appears in towns and at homes, and legend has it that he is the one who places presents of heart-shaped honey spice cakes, holy pictures, and big red apples in the children's rooms while they're asleep.

Early on Christmas Eve, children leave a letter on the windowsill for the Mother Star or the Three Wise Men to find when they deliver gifts later that evening. After dinner Star Man, probably a local priest dressed in an appropriate costume, arrives and asks each child a question from the catechism. A correct answer is rewarded with a small gift.

Card

Sending and receiving cards is a recent Polish Christmas custom. The designs combine folk motifs and religious symbols, and the verses are usually original poems written by the sender. Often a piece of *oplatek*, a thin wafer, is included in a card as a way of strengthening the bond shared by the two parties.

An early nineteenth-century Polish folk art, *wycinanki* (pronounced vi-chee-no-key), can be used to create beautiful Christmas cards. Originally, farming families cut intricate designs from black paper, with motifs including stylized birds, trees, and flowers, and used them to decorate walls, furniture, kitchen containers, and other items for the home. The *wycinanki* are cut from folded paper so that when the paper is opened up and spread flat, the design is symmetrical.

Cut a *wycinanki* design, glue it to the front of a sheet of construction paper that has been folded in half, and send or deliver the original creation as a Christmas card.

Materials:

- ✦ Construction paper, including black
- ✦ Pencil
- ✦ Glue
- ✦ Scissors
- ✦ Razor blade
- ✦ Markers
- ✦ Pictures or examples of *wycinanki* cuttings

Method:

If possible, locate pictures or examples of *wycinanki* cuttings. Study the detail in the designs as well as the subject matter represented in them. Choose a design to make.

Fold a sheet of construction paper, preferably black, in half. Using a pencil, draw one-half of the design on one side of the folded paper, so that when it is cut out and opened up it will form a symmetrical design. The folded edge of the paper will be the center of the project. Shade the part of the picture that is to be cut away.

Using the drawing as a guide, carefully cut out the *wycinanki* design. Fine cuts can be made with manicure scissors, a sharp pointed hobby knife, or a razor blade. Open the paper out flat.

Fold a sheet of construction paper in half to form a card. Use a color that will contrast with the *wycinanki* design. Glue the cutting to the front of the card.

Write a verse inside of the card and give it as a special Christmas greeting.

Crafts

For many nights before Christmas Polish families gather in their homes to create handmade ornaments to hang on their trees. Each member of the household contributes to the preparations. Adults teach traditions and children learn new skills. Although much time is involved in the process, there is little investment of money since available materials are used. Each person's individual talents combine to produce unique items of beauty.

Directions for two of the many traditional Polish ornaments are provided. Try making several of each of them to use as decorations for a tree or to give as gifts.

Polish Stars

Simple circles of paper are used to create ornaments that resemble beautiful stars.

Materials:

- ✧ Paper or foil   ✧ Thread, heavy
- ✧ Scissors   ✧ Embroidery needle
- ✧ Pencil   ✧ Cardboard
- ✧ Glue

Method:

For each ornament, begin by cutting ten to twelve circles four inches in diameter. Fold each circle in half and then in half again two more times. Crease the edges sharply so the outline of eight sections is formed. Unfold the circle. Draw a one inch circle in the center of it.

Cut each of the eight crease lines from the outer edge up to the center line. Wrap one segment of the circle around the top of a sharpened pencil with the lead broken off. This will form a cone. Glue the flaps together. Repeat this step for each segment of all twelve circles.

Cut a one inch circle out of the cardboard. Thread an embroidery needle with eight to ten inches of heavy carpet thread and string the ten to twelve pieces of the ornament together. Pull the needle and thread through the center of half of the circles. Each circle should face the same way. Bring the thread through the center of the cardboard disc and then through the remaining circle of the ornament. Make sure that the last six circles face the opposite direction from the first six.

Pull both ends of the thread together and tie them tightly near the edge of the cardboard circle. The points will spread into a ball. Use the remaining thread as a loop for hanging the star on the tree.

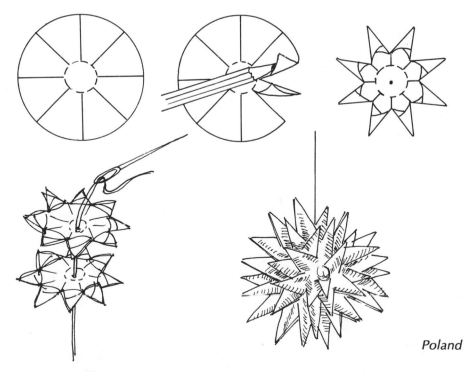

Swiat (World)

Because of its many sections and its spherical shape, the ornament known as the *swiat* is commonly called the world. Traditionally it was made from the *oplatek*, the thin Christmas wafer, but it is currently constructed out of construction paper, cardboard, or foil. When it was formed from the *oplatek*, it demanded great respect and after the tree was taken down it was hung from the ceiling for the members of the household to enjoy during the coming year.

Materials:

- ✧ Construction paper, posterboard, or foil
- ✧ Scissors
- ✧ Thread
- ✧ Embroidery needle

Method:

Cut three equal circles from construction paper, posterboard, or foil. They may be the same or different colors. Follow the illustrations and cut the indicated lines on each circle. Fold circle A in half and insert it through the center slot of circle B. Unfold A. Fold A and B so that the cut slots line up. Insert the two folded circles through C. Unfold the circles and arrange them to form a ball.

Make a hanger for the ornament. Thread an embroidery needle and bring the needle and thread through the edge of one of the circles. Knot the loop and cut off the thread. The ornament is ready to place on the tree.

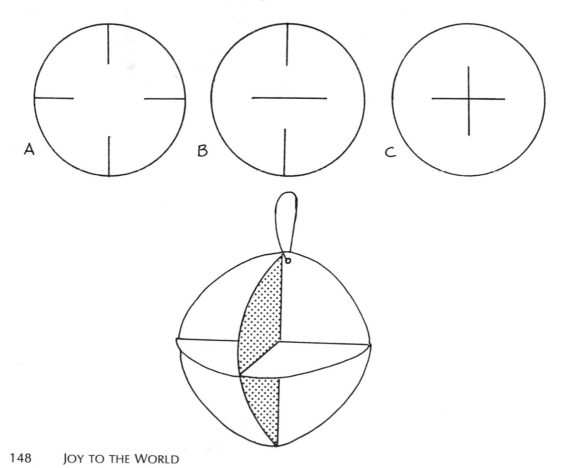

Carols

An extensive collection of Polish Christmas songs and hymns is contained in the book *Treasured Polish Christmas Customs and Traditions* (Minneapolis: Polanie Publishing Company, 1972). Over fifty carols, complete with accompaniment, traditional tunes, and new arrangements are included. Most of the songs are printed with English and Polish words.

Two songs to look for are "Christ, the King, Is Born" and "Infant Holy, Infant Lowly."

Story

The Christmas Spider, by Loretta Holz and Charles Mikolaycak (New York: Philomel Books, 1980) is a traditional Polish yuletide puppet play that tells the legend of the spider's gift to the Christ child. The tale explains the reason the Polish people consider the spider to be a symbol of good fortune. The book contains a script, directions for making the puppets and the puppet theater, and tips on staging the show.

Culinary

On the day of Christmas Eve Polish families observe *Wigilia*. They practice the tradition of keeping a vigil, fasting and abstaining from meat since it is the day before a holy day. However, the appearance of the first star in the sky on Christmas Eve marks the end of the Advent fast and starts the beginning of the Christmas feast.

Many Polish customs are associated with this meal. A few wisps of straw are laid under the table and beneath the tablecloth as a reminder of the stable at Bethlehem. A place is set at the table and kept vacant for the Christ child, whose spirit is believed to be in the room. This spot may also be prepared for a passing traveler or in honor of a departed loved one.

Oplatek, a thin, white, oblong wafer stamped with a nativity scene, is broken and shared with family and friends before the meal begins. The tradition originates from breaking bread during the mass; it is seen as a way of strengthening ties between all Polish people.

The meatless dinner may include as many as twelve courses, commemorating the twelve apostles, and highlight delicacies like borscht, pike with saffron, carp with prunes or raisins, noodles with poppy seeds, dumplings with sauerkraut and mushrooms, and a variety of desserts.

December 25, Christmas Day, is a time spent with immediate family. Typical dishes served at the noon meal are hunter's stew, polish sausage, baked ham, and breads. Extended family and friends join in the celebration on December 26. A honey spice cake, called *piernik*, which was baked early in December, is shared at this time.

Taste two of the delicacies of Poland by trying the recipes provided.

Polish Sausage With Sauerkraut

Ingredients:

- 1 pound smoked Polish sausage
- 1 32-ounce jar sauerkraut, drained
- Salt
- Pepper
- 1 teaspoon caraway seeds
- 2 slices bacon, diced
- 1 teaspoon finely chopped onion
- 2 tablespoons flour

Method:

Place Polish sausage in a shallow pan; add a small amount of water and cook in a 350 degree oven for about one hour. If water still remains, place pan on top of range and saute until the sausage is lightly browned and water evaporates.

Rinse sauerkraut with water; drain well. Place sauerkraut in a pan and cover with water; add salt, pepper, and caraway seeds. Simmer about thirty minutes. Saute bacon and onion together in a skillet, until bacon is almost crisp and onion is soft. Stir in flour. If necessary, drain some of the water from sauerkraut; stir in bacon mixture. Cut browned sausage into one inch pieces; combine with sauerkraut.

Makes four to six servings.

Kolacky

Ingredients:

- 1 cup butter
- 1 8-ounce package cream cheese
- 1/4 teaspoon vanilla extract
- 1/2 teaspoon salt
- 2 1/4 cups all purpose flour
- Thick jam or canned fruit filling, such as apricot or prune
- Powdered sugar

Method:

Cream butter and cream cheese until fluffy. Add vanilla. Add salt and flour to butter mixture, blending well. Cover and refrigerate dough several hours.

Roll out dough on lightly floured surface to 3/8 inch thickness. Cut circles two inches in diameter or larger. Place on ungreased baking sheets. Make a thumbprint about 1/4 inch deep in each cookie and fill with jam. Bake at 350 degrees until light brown, twelve to fifteen minutes. Dust with powdered sugar.

Makes about forty cookies.

Game

Polish children play games at school, at parties, and at home. The game "Running Fox" is one of their favorites.

Invite the children to stand in a circle facing inward, shoulder to shoulder, with their hands behind their backs. Select one person to be the fox. Give the fox a handkerchief to carry. Instruct the fox to walk around the outside of the circle several times, repeating this rhyme:

> The poor old fox who wanders the land,
> He has no foot, he has no hand!
> What a sad and sorry sight is he.
> We'll tan his hide with sympathy!

Tell the fox to surprise one of the children by dropping the handkerchief into his or her hands. The child who receives the hanky is to bump his or her neighbor on the right. The person who was bumped must run around the circle to avoid being touched with the hanky. The person with the handkerchief runs after the fleeing person and attempts to touch him or her with the cloth. The hanky must be kept in the hand. It cannot be thrown. If the person is touched, he or she becomes the fox in the next game. If the running person returns to his or her place in the circle without being touched, the person left holding the handkerchief becomes the fox.

▪SWEDEN▪

Country Information

*T*he Kingdom of Sweden is a country the size and shape of the state of California. It shares the Scandinavian Peninsula with Norway, is bordered by Finland on the northeast, and is separated from Denmark and the European continent by the Baltic Straits. Sweden's capital is Stockholm. The country's terrain is generally flat or rolling.

Sweden's population numbers eight and a half million. The country's largest ethnic minorities include Finns and Lapps, and there are many immigrants from Norway, Denmark, Yugoslavia, Turkey, and Iran. Sweden has one of the world's highest life expectancies and one of the lowest birth rates.

The majority of the population practice the Lutheran religion. Other major faiths include Roman Catholic, Pentecostal, Mission Covenant, Baptist, and Jewish.

Sweden's primary industries are agriculture, fishing, forestry, mining, and manufacturing.*

---

* Adams, Juanita, Editor. *Background Notes: Sweden*. Washington, D.C.: United States Department of State, 1989.

Flag

Sweden's flag, a medium blue field, has a yellow cross laid horizontally on it.

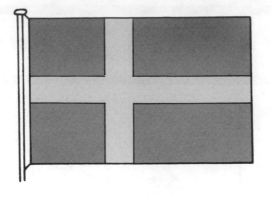

Greetings

The Christmas greeting in Swedish is *God Jul*. The greeting of peace is *fred*.

Customs

December 13, Santa Lucia Day, marks the official beginning of the Christmas season in Sweden. Early in the morning, parents are awakened by the sound of happy young voices singing "Santa Lucia" to the melody of an Italian boat song. The oldest daughter, dressed in a gown of white and wearing a crown of holly decorated with candles, carries a tray of Santa Lucia buns. The younger children in the family, carrying bright stars, follow and bring coffee.

Santa Lucia Day originated from a pagan holiday celebrating the return of more hours of daylight in the dark Swedish winter. Today the holiday is associated with the story of a Sicilian maiden who gave her life for her faith and became known as Santa Lucia. She was a Christian who used all that she owned, even her dowry, to bring bread to the poor.

During the days preceeding Christmas everything in the house is scrubbed, scoured, polished, and washed.

The Christmas tree is put up on December 23.

In Sweden, animals are included in the celebration of Christmas. Poles with sheaves of grain are put up for the birds. Cattle and horses receive a good brushing and an extra portion of oats or barley. Fish and game are given the gift of having traps and nets removed for the season.

On December 24, church bells ring and the "peace of Christmas" begins. People attend church and visit the cemetery to leave flowers and candles. At home, after dinner, the candles on the tree are lighted, the family circles it, holds hands, sings carols, and reads the Christmas story from the Bible. Gifts are opened.

Christmas Day, December 25, is a quiet family day that begins with a solemn early morning church service. Lighted candles placed in farmhouse windows shine across the path of the horses carrying sleigh loads of worshippers. The sleighs are lighted by torches, too, and when the people arrive at church, the torches are thrown into a giant bonfire. Inside the church, hundreds of candles illuminate the sanctuary.

December 26, a legal holiday, is a time for visiting, partying, and skiing.

Crèche

In keeping with the Swedish people's use of natural materials, construct a nativity set out of acorns and pinecones.*

Materials:

- ✧ Acorns
- ✧ Pinecones
- ✧ Knife
- ✧ Glue
- ✧ Scissors
- ✧ Construction paper
- ✧ Fabric scraps
- ✧ Yarn
- ✧ Permanent markers
- ✧ Straw

Method:

Decide how many figures will be made for the nativity scene. The set could include Mary, Joseph, shepherds, magi, angels, and baby Jesus.

Use a serrated knife or saw to cut the pinecones in half. For each crèche figure, glue an acorn on top of a pinecone half. Allow the pieces to dry thoroughly.

Decorate the figures with cloth, construction paper, and yarn. Cut a circular strip of fabric for each costume. Wrap a piece of material around each pinecone and glue it in place. Small pieces of yarn may be glued to the tops of the acorns to form hair. Triangles can be cut and glued to the hair to make headpieces.

Cut arms from construction paper and glue them to the top portion of the costumes.

Eyes or other facial features may be drawn on the acorns with permanent marker.

Make the baby Jesus by wrapping a small piece of cloth or paper around an acorn. Glue it in place.

Create a nativity scene on a table or in a box. Spread out the straw and set the figures on it.

---

* Shoemaker, Kathryn. *Creative Christmas: Simple Crafts From Many Lands*. Minneapolis: Winston Press, 1978.

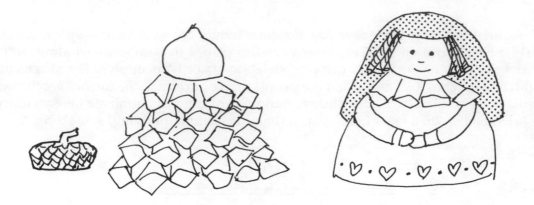

Gift Giver

In Sweden gifts are delivered to children by a little gnome called *Tomten*. *Tomten*, a good natured elf, has short legs and a long beard. He wears a bright red tasseled cap. *Tomten* is seldom seen, but he can be coaxed into a house by leaving a bowl of rice pudding on the doorstep. *Julbrock* is the name of the goat that *Tomten* rides.

Card

Swedish families even remember the birds with a Christmas gift! On Christmas Eve, December 24, people tie grain from the fall harvest into clusters and fasten them to outdoor poles. Sometimes the bird poles are decorated with seeds, stale bread, nuts, peanut butter, suet, hardened bacon drippings, oranges, apples, popped popcorn, pinecones, and cranberries. These bundles are used as traditional decorations throughout the house as well. Share the custom by using a small bundle of grain on a greeting card.

Materials:

- ✧ Construction paper
- ✧ Sheaves of wheat or grain
- ✧ Scissors
- ✧ Glue
- ✧ Tape
- ✧ Markers
- ✧ Ribbon
- ✧ Felt scraps

Method:

Choose a piece of construction paper to use as the card and fold it in half.

Cut a few sheaves of wheat or another grain into five inch lengths. Tie them together with brightly colored ribbon. Glue or tape the bundle to the center of the front of the card. The bird poles may be decorated with fruits or nuts drawn on with marker or cut from felt and glued to the wheat.

On the inside of the card, write a verse about this special Swedish custom. Send or deliver the card to a family member or friend.

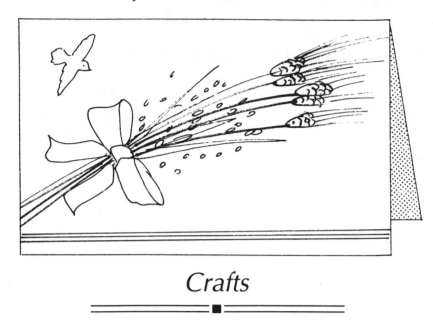

Crafts

—————■—————

Blue and yellow, the colors of the Swedish flag, are the traditional colors for many holiday decorations. Use these colors and make woven paper hearts to hang as tree ornaments.

Swedish ornaments are often made from the natural textures of grain, fiber, wood, and greenery. Stars made from straw are commonly used on Christmas trees.

Directions for both of these crafts appear below.

Christmas Heart Baskets

Materials:

✦ Construction paper   ✦ Pencil
(blue and yellow)   ✦ Glue
✦ Scissors

Method:

Cut each color of construction paper to a three inch by eight inch rectangle and fold each piece in half.

Use a pencil to draw a dotted line one inch from the unfolded end of each rectangle. Hold both pieces together and cut a rounded arch on the open end above this line. Be sure both pieces are the same size.

Beginning at the fold, cut two slits one inch from each side of each paper. Cut up to the dotted line on each slit. The paper will be divided into three equal strips.

Weave the three strips of each paper through each other to form a heart shape. Carefully open the basket and smooth out the weaving.

Cut a one-half inch by five inch strip of construction paper and glue it to the top of the basket to form a handle.

The completed Christmas heart basket may be filled with candies and nuts and hung on the tree.

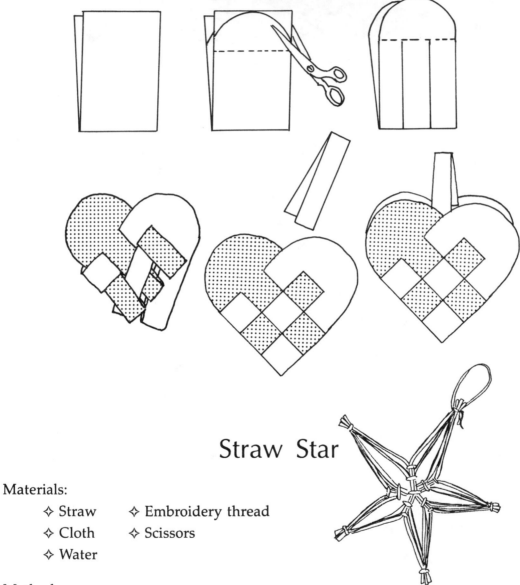

Straw Star

Materials:

- ✧ Straw
- ✧ Cloth
- ✧ Water
- ✧ Embroidery thread
- ✧ Scissors

Method:

Wrap the straw in a damp cloth the day before using it so that it will bend easily.

For each ornament, cut ten seven-inch pieces of straw. Use a piece of embroidery thread and tie the bundle together in the middle with a very tight knot. Wrap the thread around the straw twice before tying it. Take four of the pieces of straw and tie them one-half inch from the center of the ornament. Repeat four times with the remaining sixteen pieces. Tie the two middle straws of each bundle of four together one-half inch from the previous knot. Tie each point of the star together one-half inch from its end. Attach a loop of embroidery thread onto one point of the star to use as the hanger for the ornament.

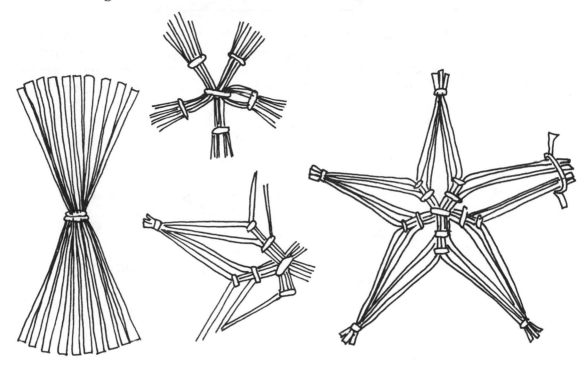

Carols

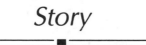

Swedish carols include "Santa Lucia" which recounts the story of the December 13th festival. Hymnals from the Covenant and Lutheran denominations are sources of additional seasonal songs, including "Joy Bells Are Ringing" and "Now Shine a Thousand Candles Bright."

Story

The Legend of the Christmas Rose, by Selma Lagerlof (Retold by Ellin Greene, illustrations by Charles Mikolaycak. New York: Holiday House, 1990), tells the story of an exiled outlaw's wife who agrees to reveal the secret of Goinge Forest to an elderly monk in hope of getting her husband pardoned.

On Christmas Eve, Robber Mother and her family take the abbot and a lay brother to the forest to witness its transformation into a beautiful garden. This miracle occurs in remembrance of the birth of the Christ child. Although the hardened heart of the lay brother causes the beauty to disappear, the Christmas rose continues to bloom every year to serve as a reminder that faith can make miracles happen.

Culinary

In Swedish homes, the Christmas Eve meal begins in the kitchen. The family gathers to dip bread into a pot of drippings from ham, pork, sausage, or corned beef which is simmering on the stove. Slices of bread are speared on forks and immersed into the liquid in remembrance of a time of famine when dark bread and broth were the only foods available.

From the kitchen, the family proceeds to the dining room for the Christmas Eve supper. This special meal is a smorgasbord of cheeses, breads, brown beans, boiled potatoes, pickled herring, fruit soup, ham, lutefish, meatballs, twenty to thirty varieties of cookies, and coffee.

Try these two traditional Swedish recipes during the Christmas season.

Santa Lucia Buns

December 13, Santa Lucia Day, marks the beginning of the Christmas season in Sweden. The oldest girl in each home dresses in a white gown and wears a wreath of holly and candles in her hair. She serves her parents special buns early in the morning.

Ingredients:

- ✦ 2 packages dry yeast
- ✦ 1/2 cup warm water
- ✦ 1 cup warm milk
- ✦ 1/4 cup honey
- ✦ 1 teaspoon ground cardamom
- ✦ Saffron, pinch

- ✦ 1 1/2 teaspoons salt
- ✦ 1/2 cup butter
- ✦ 2 eggs
- ✦ 6 to 7 cups unbleached white flour
- ✦ Raisins, optional
- ✦ 1 egg white

Method:

Combine yeast and warm water in a bowl. In another large bowl, combine milk, honey, spices, and salt. Add butter, eggs, and the yeast mixture. Beat in enough flour to make a stiff dough. Turn out onto a lightly floured surface and knead until smooth, about ten minutes. Place in a greased bowl, cover lightly with a towel and allow the mixture to rise in a warm place for about one hour, or until doubled in bulk.

When doubled, turn out again onto a lightly floured surface and knead for three minutes. Return to the bowl, cover, and let rise again for forty-five minutes.

Turn onto a floured surface, punch down, and knead for three to five minutes. Lightly cover the dough with a towel and let it rest for fifteen minutes.

Divide the dough into two dozen pieces and roll each piece into a rope about twelve inches long. Place each strand on a greased baking sheet and coil it into an S-shape. Continue to coil each end until it resembles a snail shell. A raisin may be placed in the center of each roll.

Brush the tops lightly with egg white. Bake at 350 degrees for fifteen to twenty minutes or until brown. Makes two dozen rolls.

Scandinavian Ginger Cookies

Ingredients:

- ✧ 2 egg yolks
- ✧ 1/4 cup honey
- ✧ 2/3 cup whole wheat flour
- ✧ 1/4 cup potato starch or cornstarch
- ✧ 1/2 teaspoon ground ginger
- ✧ 1/2 teaspoon ground cloves
- ✧ 1/2 teaspoon cinnamon
- ✧ 1 teaspoon baking powder
- ✧ 2 tablespoons heavy cream
- ✧ 3 tablespoons butter, melted
- ✧ 1 teaspoon vanilla

Method:

Beat together the egg yolks and honey. Mix the whole wheat flour, potato starch (cornstarch), ginger, ground cloves, cinnamon, and baking powder. Add half of the flour mixture to the egg yolks. Add the cream and butter. Stir in the vanilla and the remaining flour mixture. Mix thoroughly.

Grease a baking sheet. Preheat the oven to 350 degrees. Drop the cookies onto the baking sheet. Flatten with the tines of a fork. Bake for ten minutes, or until cooked through. Cool on a rack. Store in an airtight container.

Makes about thirty-six cookies.

Game

Christmas Eve dinner in Swedish households includes a game of finding an almond that has been hidden in a bowl of rice pudding. It is most fun if the person who locates the nut keeps the discovery a secret until all have finished their treat. Traditionally, the person who retrieves the almond will marry in the coming year or will have an especially prosperous year. Often the finder receives a gift, which may be a fat marzipan candy pig!

Try a recipe for rice pudding, add an almond, and play the game.

Rice Pudding

Ingredients:

- ✧ 2 eggs, well beaten
- ✧ 1/2 cup sugar
- ✧ 1/4 teaspoon salt
- ✧ 2 cups milk, scalded
- ✧ 1 1/4 cups cooked, cooled rice

- ✧ 1 cup raisins
- ✧ l teaspoon vanilla
- ✧ Cinnamon
- ✧ Nutmeg
- ✧ Almond

Method:

Combine eggs, sugar, and salt. Gradually add scalded milk. Add rice, raisins, vanilla, cinnamon, nutmeg, and one almond.

Pour into greased one quart casserole. Set in a shallow pan; pour hot water into the pan one inch deep. Bake in a 325 degree oven for 1 1/2 hours.

Makes four to six servings.

BIBLIOGRAPHY

Alessi, Vince. *Programs for Advent and Christmas.* Valley Forge, PA: Judson Press, 1978.

Background Notes. Washington, D.C.: United States Department of State, Various Dates.

Bragdon, Allen D., editor, produced in cooperation with the United States Committee for UNICEF. *Joy Through the World.* New York: Dodd, Mead, 1985.

Brink, Emily R., editor. *Psalter Hymnal.* Grand Rapids, MI: CRC Publications, 1987.

Christmas: An American Annual of Christmas Literature and Art, Volume 49. Minneapolis: Augsburg, 1979.

Christmas in Britain. Chicago: World Book, 1978.

Christmas in France. Chicago: World Book - Childcraft International, Inc., 1980.

Christmas in Mexico. Chicago: World Book, 1976.

Christmas in the Netherlands. Chicago: World Book - Childcraft International, Inc., 1981.

Christmas in Poland. Chicago: World Book, 1989.

Christmas in Scandinavia. Chicago: World Book Encyclopedia, 1977.

Christmas: The Annual of Christmas Literature and Art, Volume 59. Minneapolis: Augsburg, 1989.

Coskey, Evelyn. *Christmas Crafts for Everyone.* Nashville: Abingdon, 1976.

The Covenant Hymnal. Chicago: Covenant Press, 1973.

Cracchiolo, Rachelle and Mary Dupuy Smith. *Christmas Ornaments From Around the World.* Sunset Beach, CA: Teacher Created Materials, 1977.

Cusack, Margaret. *The Christmas Carol Sampler.* San Diego: Harcourt Brace Jovanovich, 1983.

Davidson, Linda S., editor. *Creative Ideas for Advent, Volume 3.* Brea, CA: Educational Ministries, Inc., 1990.

Davidson, Robert G., editor. *Creative Ideas for Advent, Volume 1.* Brea, CA: Educational Ministries, Inc., 1980.

Davidson, Robert G. and Linda S., editors. *Creative Ideas for Advent, Volume 2.* Brea, CA: Educational Ministries, Inc., 1986.

Ehret, Walter and George K. Evans. *The International Book of Christmas Carols.* Brattleboro, VT: Stephen Greene Press, 1980.

Erickson, Joyce. *In Straw and Story: Christmas Resources for Home and Church.* Elgin, IL: Brethren Press, 1983.

Fiarotta, Phyllis and Noel. *Confetti: The Kids' Make-It-Yourself, Do-It-Yourself Party Book.* New York: Workman, 1978.

Fowler, Virginia. *Christmas Crafts and Customs Around the World.* New York: Prentice-Hall, 1984.

Have a Natural Christmas '86. Emmaus, PA: Rodale Press, 1986.

Henderson, Kathy. *Christmas Trees.* Chicago: Children's Press, 1989.

Herda, D. J. *Christmas.* New York: Franklin Watts, 1983.

Ickis, Marguerite. *Book of Festivals and Holidays the World Over.* New York: Dodd, Mead, 1970.

Ideals Christmas Around the World. Milwaukee: Ideals, 1981.

Ideals: Christmas Issue. Volume 31, Number 6. Milwaukee: Ideals, 1974.

Ideals Family Christmas Book. Milwaukee: Ideals, 1973.

Jackson, Kathryn. *The Joys of Christmas: Christmas Customs and Legends Around the World*. New York: Golden Press, 1976.

Johnson, Lois. *Christmas Stories 'Round the World*. Chicago: Rand McNally, 1970.

Kelley, Emily. *Christmas Around the World*. Minneapolis: Carolrhoda Books, 1986.

Lathrop, Carolynne & Gordon. *Christmas in All the World*. Minneapolis: Augsburg, 1979.

Lubin, Leonard B. *Christmas Gift-Bringers*. New York: Lothrop, Lee and Shepard, 1989.

Magos, Eunice M. and Esther H. Hornnes. *Learning Journeys*. Laguna Niguel, CA: The Monkey Sisters, 1985.

Mead, Arden W. *Repeat the Sounding Joy: Advent Meditations on the Great Carols of Christmas*. St. Louis, MO: Creative Communications for the Parish, 1988.

Mead, Peter. "Joy To The World." St. Louis, MO: Creative Communications for the Parish, 1990.

Metcalfe, Edna. *The Trees of Christmas*. Nashville: Abingdon, 1969.

Meyer, Carolyn. *Christmas Crafts: Things to Make the 24 Days Before Christmas*. New York: Harper & Row, 1974.

Noble, T. Tertius. *A Round of Carols*. New York: Henry Z. Walck, Inc., n.d.

Polon, Linda and Aileen Cantwell. *The Whole Earth Holiday Book*. Glenview, IL: Scott, Foresman & Company, 1983.

Posselt, Eric, editor. *World's Greatest Christmas Stories*. Chicago: Ziff-Davis, 1949.

The Presbyterian Hymnal. Louisville: Westminster/John Knox Press, 1990.

Purdy, Susan. *Christmas Cooking Around the World*. New York: Franklin Watts, 1983.

Schlabach, Joetta Handrich. *Extending the Table . . . A World Community Cookbook*. Scottdale, PA: Herald Press, 1991.

Schuman, Jo Miles. *Art From Many Hands*. Worcester, MA: Davis Publications, 1981.

Shoemaker, Kathryn. *Creative Christmas: Simple Crafts From Many Lands*. Minneapolis: Winston Press, 1978.

Spicer, Dorothy Gladys. *46 Days of Christmas*. New York: Coward-McCann, Inc., 1960.

Stewart, Stan and Pauline. *Nothing! But Ideas . . . On Christmas and Advent*. Perth, West Australia: Treking, 1983.

Tonn, Maryjane Hooper, editor. *Ideals Christmas*. Volume 29, Number 6. Milwaukee: Ideals, 1972.

Treasured Polish Christmas Customs and Traditions. Minneapolis: Polanie Publishing Company, 1972.

Warren, Jean and Elizabeth McKinnon. *Small World Celebrations*. Everett, WA: Warren Publishing House, 1988.

Wernecke, Herbert H. *Christmas Customs Around the World*. Philadelphia: Westminster Press, 1979.

Wezeman, Phyllis Vos. *Peacemaking Creatively Through the Arts*. Brea, CA: Educational Ministries, Inc., 1990.

Wezeman, Phyllis Vos and Jude Dennis Fournier. *Advent Alphabet*. Brea, CA: Educational Ministries, Inc., 1989.

Wezeman, Phyllis Vos and Jude Dennis Fournier. *Counting the Days: Twenty-Five Ways*. Brea, CA: Educational Ministries, Inc., 1989.

Wezeman, Phyllis Vos and Jude Dennis Fournier. *Symbols of the Season: Exciting Epiphany Experiences*. Brea, CA: Educational Ministries, Inc., 1991.

The World Book Encyclopedia. Volume 3 (C-Ch). Chicago: World Book, Inc., 1984.

Young, Carlton R., editor. *The United Methodist Hymnal.* Nashville: The United Methodist Publishing House, 1989.

EMBASSIES

AUSTRALIA

1601 Massachusetts Avenue NW
Washington, DC 20008

(202) 797-3000

BRAZIL

3006 Massachusetts Avenue NW
Washington, DC 20008

(202) 745-2700

CANADA

501 Pennsylvania Avenue NW
Washington, DC 20001

(202) 682-1740

ECUADOR

2535 15th Street NW
Washington, DC 20009

(202) 234-7200

GERMANY

4645 Reservoir Road NW
Washington, DC 20007

(202) 298-4000

INDIA

2107 Massachusetts Avenue NW
Washington, DC 20008

(202) 939-7000

JAPAN

2520 Massachusetts Avenue NW
Washington, DC 20008

(202) 939-6700

MEXICO

1911 Pennsylvania Avenue NW
Washington, DC 20006

(202) 728-1600

NETHERLANDS

4200 Linnean Avenue NW
Washington, DC 20008

(202) 244-5300

NIGERIA

2201 M Street NW
Washington, DC 20037

(202) 822-1500

POLAND

2640 16th Street NW
Washington, DC 20009

(202) 234-3800, 3801, 3802

SWEDEN

600 New Hampshire Avenue NW Suite 1200
Washington, DC 20037

(202) 944-5600